FRUIT OF THE SPIRIT

LOVE

JOY

PEACE

FRUIT OF THE SPIRIT

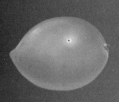
PATIENCE

48 *Bible Studies*
FOR INDIVIDUALS OR GROUPS

GENTLENESS

PHYLLIS J. LePEAU · JACK KUHATSCHEK · JACALYN EYRE
STEPHEN EYRE · PETER SCAZZERO

KINDNESS

FAITHFULNESS

SELF-CONTROL

ZONDERVAN®

ZONDERVAN.com/
AUTHORTRACKER
follow your favorite authors

ZONDERVAN

Fruit of the Spirit

This title is also available as a Zondervan ebook.
Visit www.zondervan.com/ebooks.

Faithfulness
Copyright © 2001 by Jacalyn Eyre

This title is also available as a Zondervan ebook.
Visit www.zondervan.com/ebooks.

Gentleness
Copyright © 2001 by Phyllis J. LePeau

Joy
Copyright © 2001 by Phyllis J. LePeau

Kindness
Copyright © 2001 by Phyllis J. LePeau

Love
Copyright © 2001 by Peter Scazzero

Patience
Copyright © 2001 by Stephen Eyre

This title is also available as a Zondervan ebook.
Visit www.zondervan.com/ebooks.

Peace
Copyright © 2001 by Jack Kuhatschek

Self-Control
Copyright © 2001 by Jack Kuhatschek

Requests for information should be addressed to:

Zondervan, *Grand Rapids, Michigan 49530*

ISBN 978-0-310-69845-6

Study 25 is adapted from a study in *Caring for Physical Needs* in the Caring People Series from InterVarsity Press and is used by permission.

Cover design: Chris Tobias / Tobias Outerwear for Books
Interior design: David Conn

Printed in the United States of America

20 21 22 23 24 /DCI/ 55 54 53

Contents

PATIENCE: THE BENEFITS OF WAITING

KINDNESS: REACHING OUT TO OTHERS

FAITHFULNESS: THE FOUNDATION OF TRUE FRIENDSHIP

GENTLENESS: THE STRENGTH OF BEING TENDER

SELF-CONTROL: MASTERING OUR PASSIONS

How to Use This Study

"The fruit of the Spirit is love, joy, peace, forbearance [patience], kindness, goodness, faithfulness, gentleness and self-control. Against such things there is no law." (Galatians 5:22 – 23)

Every Christ follower aspires to a life defined by these character traits. Yet living them out is as much a challenge today as it was when the apostle Paul addressed them to the believers in Galatia two thousand years ago — and possible, now as then, only when one walks daily in step with God's Spirit.

This study was written to help you do just that: to allow the Spirit of God to use the Word of God to produce his fruit in your life. First published as eight individual studies more than twenty years ago, the content has benefited more than a half million men and women as they've sought to grow in their Christian faith. While the children of the five authors have become adults with children of their own, the truths presented are as fresh and relevant as ever.

To get the most from this study, you need to understand a few basic facts:

- It is designed to be flexible. You can use it in your individual quiet times or for group discussion (small groups, neighborhood Bible studies, etc.).
- It is organized chronologically based on the Galatians 5 passage — starting with love and ending with self-control (kindness and goodness are treated as a single entity). You can study the fruit of the Spirit in any order that is best for you or your group. There are six studies per trait.
- Each of the forty-eight studies deliberately focuses on only one or two passages. That allows you to see each passage in its context, avoiding the

temptation of proof texting and the frustration of "Bible hopscotch" (jumping from verse to verse). If you would like to look up additional passages, a Bible concordance will give the most help.

- The questions help you *discover* what the Bible says rather than simply *telling* you what it says. They encourage you to think and to explore options rather than to merely fill in the blanks with one-word answers.

- "Resource boxes" accompany some of the questions to enrich your time in God's Word. These helps include explanations of words from the original biblical languages, cultural or historical notes, pertinent quotations from Bible scholars, and comments from the author of the study.

- An "approach" question ("Warming Up"), prayer suggestions, and application ideas are also provided for each study. The approach question is designed to reveal where your thoughts or feelings might need to be transformed by Scripture. Thus it is best to answer it *before* reading the passage.

SUGGESTIONS FOR INDIVIDUAL STUDY

1. Begin each study with prayer. Ask God to help you understand the passage and apply it to your life.

2. A good modern translation, such as the New International Version, the English Standard Version, or the New Living Translation, will give you the most help. However, the questions in this guide are based on the New International Version.

3. Read and reread the passage(s). You must know what the passage says before you can understand what it means and how it applies to you.

4. Write your answers in the space provided. This will help you to clearly express your understanding of the passage.

5. Keep a Bible dictionary handy. Use it to look up any unfamiliar words, names, or places.

SUGGESTIONS FOR GROUP STUDY

1. Come to the study prepared. Careful preparation will greatly enrich your time in group discussion.

2. Be willing to join in the discussion or to encourage discussion if you are leading the group. Plan to share what God has taught you in your individual study.

3. Stick to the passage being studied. Base your answers on the verses being
   discussed rather than on outside authorities such as commentaries or your
   favorite author or speaker.

4. Try to be sensitive to the other members of the group. Listen attentively
   when they speak, and be affirming whenever you can. This will encourage
   more hesitant members of the group to participate.

5. Be careful not to dominate the discussion. By all means, participate! But
   allow others to have equal time.

Love

BUILDING LASTING RELATIONSHIPS

Peter Scazzero

Introduction

In the film entitled *Cipher in the Snow*, a young school-age child is waiting for a school bus on a cold January morning. The other children are playing and laughing with one another, while Roger stands alone, staring at the ground. When the bus arrives, he is the last one to climb the steps. While others talk and joke together, Roger sits alone behind the bus driver. After a few miles, Roger stands up, drops his books, and leans on a metal pole to steady himself. Finally, the bus driver pulls over to the side of the road and opens the door. Roger staggers out into the roadside and falls into the snow dead.

While the autopsy sheds no light on his death, research into his life does. His parents had divorced and his mother remarried. His new stepfather resented Roger's intrusion into their marriage. His mother spent almost no time with him.

As a result, he began withdrawing from other friends at school and became apathetic toward his schoolwork. Slowly, Roger built around himself a world of silence. Both teachers and friends eventually grew tired of entering that world.

In only a few months, everything and everyone of value to Roger had been either lost or taken from him. With no place of shelter and no words of encouragement, he felt like a cipher—an empty zero. This sensitive child was unable to stand the pain for long. Roger was not killed by an infirmity or a wound. He was killed by a lack of words of love and acceptance.[1]

---

1. See Gary Smalley and John Trent, *The Blessing* (Nashville: Thomas Nelson, 1986), 55–58.

This powerful story illustrates the deep human need within each of us to receive love from others. Many of the believers and visitors who attend our churches are like Roger. They are desperately lonely and searching for genuine relationships. They come with a profound need for love and acceptance from the Lord Jesus and from us.

This section of *Fruit of the Spirit* explores the mysterious and many-faceted nature of love from a biblical perspective. The ultimate goal of these six studies is to allow the world to see God and to experience his love through us. As the apostle John writes, "No one has ever seen God; but if we love one another, God lives in us and his love is made complete [literally, 'comes to full expression'] in us" (1 John 4:12).

A few hours before going to the cross, Jesus prayed, "Righteous Father ... I have made you known to them, and will continue to make you known *in order that the love you have for me may be in them*" (John 17:25 – 26, italics added). As you consider what the Bible says about love, may that fruit of the Spirit overflow in your life toward the Lord Jesus, his church, and the world.

Loving Jesus

LUKE 7:36–50

In the book *Too Busy Not to Pray*, Bill Hybels writes, "To people in the fast lane, determined to make it on their own, prayer is an embarrassing interruption.... Where does the still, small voice of God fit into our hectic lives? When do we allow him to lead and guide and correct and affirm? And if this seldom or never happens, how can we lead truly authentic Christian lives?"[1]

God calls every believer first to himself and then to ministry. One of the greatest dangers facing us today is our tendency to be so involved in various activities that we lose that "sincere and pure devotion to Christ" spoken about by the apostle Paul (2 Corinthians 11:3). God wants us to be filled with passion and love for his Son, Jesus Christ.

This story of Jesus and the sinful woman illustrates the kind of simple devotion that God desires.

WARMING UP

1. Think of a person who has "fallen in love." How are his or her attitudes, priorities, and other relationships affected?

---

1. Bill Hybels, *Too Busy Not to Pray* (Downers Grove, Ill.: InterVarsity Press, 1988), 7, 99.

DIGGING IN

2. Read Luke 7:36–50. How would you describe the setting of this story (the place, the people present, the atmosphere, and so on)?

3. In what ways does the woman demonstrate lavish devotion to Jesus (vv. 36–38)?

> It was normal to anoint a person's head with olive oil, a cheap and plentiful substance in Jesus' day, but this woman uses an alabaster jar of perfume (something very expensive) and anoints his feet. She is apparently so overwhelmed with emotions of joy and repentance that she cannot contain herself.
>
> **I. Howard Marshall, *Commentary on Luke*,
> New International Greek Testament Commentary**

4. Imagine yourself at Simon the Pharisee's dinner table. What might you feel during this woman's interruption?

    Why do you think her actions offend Simon (v. 39)?

5. In what ways could we express extravagant devotion to Jesus today?

How might that upset some people around us?

6. What does it cost this woman to publicly show her love for Jesus?

What are the costs for you?

7. What point does Jesus make for Simon in the parable of the two debtors (vv. 40 – 43)?

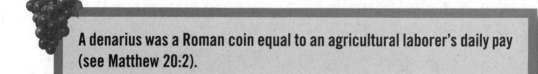

A denarius was a Roman coin equal to an agricultural laborer's daily pay (see Matthew 20:2).

8. Why does Jesus contrast Simon's hospitality with that of the woman (vv. 44 – 46)?

According to Jesus, what does it indicate when a person has little love for him (v. 47)?

9.   What further blessings does the sinful woman receive from Jesus as a result of her faith (vv. 48 – 50)?

10.   With whom do you relate more: Simon the Pharisee, who knows the Bible and is very active for God, or this woman, who loves God with reckless abandon? Explain.

Simon, like the elder brother in the parable of the prodigal son, was moral and respectable. The problem, however, as the eighteenth-century preacher and evangelist George Whitefield said, is that these are "damnable good works" because we can easily rely on our "record" or performance for God's love versus the record and performance of Jesus on our behalf. The insidious problem with respectability and goodness is that we can subtly become convinced God owes us because we obey him!

11.   Why is a passionate love for Jesus so vital if we are to have healthy, loving relationships with others?

12. What obstacles in your life are hindering you from a single-minded devotion to Jesus?

PRAY ABOUT IT

Take a few minutes now to focus your heart and mind on Jesus in prayer, expressing words of affection and adoration to him. Then ask God to help your love for him to be as lavish as his forgiveness.

TAKING THE NEXT STEP

Before people die, they often share the concerns greatest on their hearts. In John 17 we read Jesus' final words prior to his death. The end of this magnificent prayer climaxes in Jesus praying that the love the Father has for him might be in us. Meditate on and memorize John 17:26. Imagine the perfect, pure love of the Father toward his Son, Jesus, and then imagine yourself loving Jesus with that kind of love. In the coming days, pray for God to give you the love he has for Jesus. You can be sure God will answer that prayer! He is eager for us to integrate that kind of prayer into our devotional lives.

STUDY 2

Loving God's Family

JOHN 13:1–17

Richard Foster notes the difference between choosing to be a servant and choosing to serve. When we choose to serve, we are still very much in charge. We decide whom we will serve, when we'll do it, and to what extent. We exclaim, "I won't let him walk all over me!"

Servants, on the other hand, have surrendered their right to choose who and when they will serve. All of their life is seen from the perspective of a slave. They no longer possess the rights of free men and women. They are completely available and vulnerable![1]

In John 13 Jesus shows us what it means to be a loving servant.

WARMING UP

1.   Is it more difficult for you to serve some people than others? Why?

---

1. See Richard Foster, *Celebration of Discipline* (New York: Harper and Row, 1978), 115 – 16.

DIGGING IN

2.   Read John 13:1 – 17. How do verses 1 – 3 set the stage for what is to follow?

3.   What three things does Jesus know (vv. 1, 3)?

      In light of this, why are Jesus' actions so extraordinary?

4.   How does knowing who you are, where you've come from, and where you're going enable you to better serve others?

5.   Imagine yourself as one of the Twelve, reclining at the table with Jesus. What might you have seen, heard, and felt as Jesus rose to wash your feet?

> The roads of Palestine were quite unsurfaced and uncleaned. In dry weather, they were inches deep in dust, and in wet weather they were liquid mud. The shoes ordinary people wore were sandals; and these sandals were simply soles held on to the foot by a few straps. They gave little protection against the dust or the mud of the roads. For that reason there were always great water pots at the door of the house; and a servant was there with a ewer and a towel to wash the soiled feet of the guests as they came in.
>
> **William Barclay, *The Gospel of John*, The Daily Bible Study Series**

6. Foot washing in Jewish eyes was something even Jewish slaves were not required to do. This was a task reserved for Gentile slaves, wives, and children. (Prior to Jesus, women and children did not hold a very esteemed place in Jewish society.) What, then, did Jesus' action demonstrate?

7. Read the dialogue between Jesus and Peter in verses 6 – 10. Why does Peter reject Jesus' ministry to him?

8. Peter is thinking of literal washings. What do you think Jesus means by his statements in verses 8 and 10?

9. Most Bible scholars see the bath as the washing of forgiveness at conversion and the foot washing as the cleansing of daily dirt (sin) we pick up along the way. How do these acts beautifully illustrate our relationship with Jesus Christ?

10. What point does Jesus powerfully drive home in verses 12 – 17?

> The term *Lord* was a revered one. If Jesus stooped to perform a slave's task for the disciples, how much more readily should they do the same for each other (see John 13:34 – 35)? Yet according to Luke 22:24, they continued arguing over who was the greatest even at the Last Supper!

11. Jesus says, "I have set you an example that you should do as I have done for you" (v. 15). How do you think Jesus expected the disciples to follow his example?

12. What does it mean today for you to "wash someone's feet"? (Give practical examples.)

13. Why do you think Jesus says that to do this will bring blessing (or happiness; v. 17)?

14. Jesus knew that Judas was a traitor and his enemy. Yet he washed his feet too. Think of one or two people who might be difficult to serve. In what practical ways might you "wash their feet" by serving them?

PRAY ABOUT IT

Pray that God would cause the servant heart of Christ to be formed in you, that you wouldn't simply do acts of a servant, but that you would *be* a servant.

TAKING THE NEXT STEP

Think through specific opportunities to serve another person, such as the common courtesy of a thank-you note, a letter or email of appreciation, a phone call of affirmation, an invitation to your home, a listening ear, or a helping hand. Begin each day by praying, "Lord Jesus, today bring into my path someone whom I can serve."

Loving Your Neighbor

LUKE 10:25–37

On March 13, 1964, Kitty Genovese, age twenty-eight, was returning home to her apartment in New York City when she was stabbed by a man in her stairwell. She screamed for help. Thirty-eight respectable, law-abiding citizens heard the cry but did nothing. The man ran off. He returned a second time, stabbing her again. There were additional screams for help. The killer returned a third and final time to silence the screams once and for all. None of the thirty-eight people wanted to get involved. By the time a few witnesses worked up the courage to make anonymous phone calls to the police, Genovese was dead.

With the breakdown of the family, the increase of AIDS and drug use, homelessness, and single-parent homes, we find ourselves surrounded by enormous needs. The temptation to retreat into ourselves and into noninvolvement is great. Jesus, in this famous parable, speaks to our struggle.

WARMING UP

1. How do you respond when you are approached by a stranger asking for money? Explain.

DIGGING IN

2. Read Luke 10:25 – 37. In verses 25 and 29, the expert in the law asks two questions. What do they reveal about him?

3. Experts in the law were the undisputed judges of the Old Testament. As a result, they were highly esteemed and honored by the common people. Why do you think this man wanted to "justify" himself (v. 29)?

> Experts in the law, or scribes, were the authoritative interpreters of the Old Testament in the days of Jesus. They claimed the positions of first rank, sought the praise of the people, and dressed in long robes to distinguish themselves (see Matthew 23:5 – 7; Mark 12:38 – 39; Luke 11:43; 20:46). They felt their study of the law entitled them to eternal life (John 5:39) and often served as judges in Jewish courts. Throughout the ministry of Jesus, they were his most vehement opponents and were unrelenting in their hatred of him (Mark 2:16; Luke 5:30).
>
> *The New International Dictionary of the Bible*

In what ways do we tend to water down God's commands in order to justify our lifestyle?

4.   The road from Jerusalem to Jericho descends about thirty-three hundred feet in the course of seventeen miles. It runs through desert and rocky country and was noted for being filled with robbers. What was the condition of the man after the robbers attacked him (v. 30)?

5.   Jericho was one of the principal residences for priests. What might be some of the reasons the priest and Levite passed by on the other side of the road?

6.   What are some of our reasons we sometimes pass by those in need?

Are there times when our reasons might be legitimate? Explain.

7.   When the Samaritan saw the man, he "took pity" (or "felt compassion," New Living Translation). This same Greek word is often used to describe Jesus' heart toward those in need. What did it cost the Samaritan to help this man (in terms of money, time, risk, and so on)?

The Greek word for "he took pity" is *splauchnizomai*. It literally means "his heart contracted convulsively" at the sight of crying human need. This word was used of Jesus when he saw that the multitudes were like sheep without a shepherd (Matthew 9:36), when he was approached by the leper for healing (Mark 1:41), and when he saw the widow at Nain mourning her son (Luke 7:13).

What do his actions the next day, when he has to resume his journey, suggest to us about him?

8. Why do you think Jesus picked a Samaritan, someone the Jews hated, as the example of someone loving his neighbor?

What ethnic or religious group, nationality, or person do you think Jesus might have chosen to make the same point to you?

9. After studying this parable, who would you say is your "neighbor"?

In what ways might it cost you to be a neighbor like this?

10. Jesus, during his brief three-year ministry, was surrounded by enormous spiritual, physical, and emotional needs, many of which he didn't meet. How do you think Jesus lived with that tension (see John 5:19 – 20; 17:4)?

11. Most of us pass by far more needs than we can possibly meet. In light of this parable and the example of Jesus, what are the key issues for us in loving our neighbor?

12. In practice, what does it mean for you to obey the command to "go and do likewise" (Luke 10:37)?

13. What long-range issues and changes in lifestyle might you need to consider? Explain.

14. Think of one person who seems to be on the side of the road like the man in this parable. How can you be a neighbor to that person?

PRAY ABOUT IT

Pray that God would give you eyes to see the preciousness and glory of those around you.

TAKING THE NEXT STEP

Read Matthew 25:31 – 46. What, according to Jesus' parable, will be the evaluation tool at judgment day to determine if our faith is authentic or not? Why do you think he uses such difficult language? In what way can you reach out to the "least of these" around you? Take specific steps to put this into practice.

STUDY 4

Love That Forgives

MATTHEW 18:21—35

"I forgive, but I don't forget."

"No, I won't tell him how much I'm hurt. He didn't even think about thanking me."

"I'm very hurt after what she said about me. I know she's sorry, but I'll never go back to that group again."

Hebrews 12:15 warns us to "see to it … that no bitter root grows up to cause trouble and defile many." Bitterness or unforgiveness is like a root hidden beneath the ground. If it is not pulled out, then it will eventually grow and bring forth bad fruit.

This root is formed from a variety of causes: broken relationships, parental neglect, unfulfilled expectations, feelings of betrayal, and so on.

An unwillingness to forgive and deal with bitter roots has enormous consequences — spiritually, emotionally, and even physically. For this reason, Jesus strongly addresses this life-and-death issue for us in Matthew 18.

WARMING UP

1. Recall a time when you, or someone you know, allowed unforgiveness or bitterness to take root. What were the consequences?

DIGGING IN

2. Read Matthew 18:21 – 35. Jewish law taught that "if a man sins once, twice, or three times, they forgive him; if he sins a fourth time, they do not forgive him" (Yoma 5.13). In light of this, what does Peter's question in verse 21 reveal about his view of forgiveness?

    What is so amazing about Jesus' reply (v. 22)?

3. Jesus expands on his answer with a parable (vv. 23 – 35). How does the servant who owes ten thousand talents (roughly equal to ten million dollars) respond when the king is ready to settle accounts?

> The debt was more than the total revenue of a wealthy province. This suggests that the servant was a person who gathered revenue for the king. The sale of the man's wife, children, and possessions would pay for only a small percentage of what he owed.
>
> Robert Mounce, *Matthew: A Good News Commentary*

How might you feel if you were under the weight of such a debt?

4. Consider the three actions the master takes toward his servant (v. 27). How do they illustrate the way God has dealt with us?

5. How do the master's actions contrast with the way the servant treats his fellow servant (vv. 28 – 30)?

6. A hundred denarii was worth about twenty dollars. What point is Jesus making about us by using such a ridiculously small amount?

7. Why do you think the servant failed to forgive after having been forgiven so much?

The parable gives us two powerful motivators for forgiving: the mercy of God and a wholesome fear of God. Fear of the Lord refers to the reverence and awe of God that lead to obedience: "The fear of the LORD is the beginning of knowledge" (Proverbs 1:7), and "to fear the LORD is to hate evil" (Proverbs 8:13). An unwillingness to forgive is a dangerous thing. When forgiveness and mercy do not flow to others, God does get angry.

8.   How does the master judge the servant when he finds out what he's done (vv. 32 – 34)?

Why do you think God's sentence against us is so severe if we don't forgive (v. 35)?

9.   Verse 34 tells us "his master handed him over to the jailers to be tortured." In what ways are we tortured when we choose not to release others from the debt they owe us?

How do we affect others when we don't forgive freely?

10.   According to Jesus, what does an unwillingness to extend mercy prove (v. 35; see also Matthew 6:15)?

11.   Think of a person who has hurt or mistreated you, whom you have had difficulty forgiving. How can a deep understanding of God's love for you radically affect your attitude?

> Forgiveness is a process, not an event. The deeper the wound, the more time needed for healing. Grieving is an important element of forgiveness. Sometimes we forgive too quickly, not allowing ourselves to feel pain. This leads to superficial, cheap forgiveness. Grieving means letting go. It is a work of grace.

12. Jesus began by saying that this is what the kingdom of God is like (Matthew 18:23). Summarize how and why Christ's kingdom is so different than the world's.

PRAY ABOUT IT

Ask for a fresh vision of God's mercy and love, and pray for help to forgive those who have hurt you.

TAKING THE NEXT STEP

Forgiving others takes a miracle. Jesus said in the Lord's Prayer (Matthew 6:9 – 13) that we are to forgive others every day, knowing this would be a challenge for all disciples throughout history. On a piece of paper, make a list of some of the betrayals and hurts you have experienced. One by one, release the items on this list to God. Ask him to heal you. Then destroy the list. Remember, the work of transformation is essential to the Christian life. Every time the pain returns, ask God to teach you through it. Pray through the Lord's Prayer on a regular basis as a reminder.

It has been said that more people have been killed with the tongue than in all the wars in human history. In the workplace, classroom, home, and even churches, complaining and faultfinding are a way of life. The Bible describes Satan as the ultimate accuser, standing before the Father day and night to point out our faults (Revelation 12:10). As a result, both the world and the church are filled with people crying out for words of affirmation and love.

James 3 explores the powerful effect of our tongues and challenges us to put our faith into action by loving one another with our words.

WARMING UP

1. Do you find it easier to speak words of encouragement and blessing to people or to criticize them? Explain.

DIGGING IN

2. Read James 3:1–12. Why does James suggest we should hesitate before becoming teachers (v. 1)?

God does indeed have a higher standard and accountability for those in leadership. A good example of this is found in 1 Timothy 5:20, where Paul says that an elder who sins should be rebuked publicly so others will be warned.

3. How do a horse's bit and a ship's rudder illustrate the power of the tongue (vv. 3–4)?

4. James compares the tongue to a fire (vv. 5–6). How does this image illustrate its potential destructiveness?

Just as fire came down from heaven at Pentecost to enable the early church to declare the wonders of God with their tongues (Acts 2:3–4), so there is a fire that comes from hell itself. This was illustrated with Peter when he rebuked Jesus, telling him not to go to the cross. Jesus replied, "Get behind me, Satan! You are a stumbling block to me; you do not have in mind the concerns of God, but merely human concerns" (Matthew 16:23).

5. When have you seen "a great forest ... set on fire" by words?

6. James points out that we can tame almost every kind of bird and beast (v. 7). Why, then, can't we tame the tongue (v. 8)?

7. How can words function as a "deadly poison" in relationships and churches?

8. James notes that the tongue can have a positive impact. What hypocrisy, however, does he expose in verses 9 – 12?

9. What is the result if both fresh and salt water should flow from the same spring (vv. 11 – 12)?

10. How is loving one another with our words related to worshiping together on Sunday?

11. Ephesians 4:29 states, "Do not let any unwholesome talk come out of your mouths, but only what is helpful for building others up according to their needs, that it may benefit those who listen." What kinds of unwholesome talk do we commonly indulge in that do not build up or benefit others?

12. What are some constructive ways you can use your tongue to bless those in your church or fellowship group?

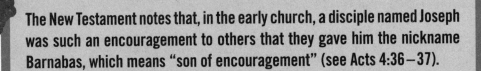

The New Testament notes that, in the early church, a disciple named Joseph was such an encouragement to others that they gave him the nickname Barnabas, which means "son of encouragement" (see Acts 4:36 – 37).

13. Think of at least three people with whom you have regular contact. What can you do to love each one with your words?

PRAY ABOUT IT

Pray Psalm 15:2 – 4. Lord, make me a person who speaks the truth from the heart, whose tongue utters no slander, who does no wrong to my neighbor, who doesn't slur others, and who honors those who fear you.

TAKING THE NEXT STEP

Every time you enter and leave a room, intentionally and warmly address people you meet with kind words. Use your tongue to set the tone and change the emotional/spiritual climate of your workplace and your home. Pray that God would be the "aroma of Christ" (2 Corinthians 2:15) through your words.

Read and meditate on the following verses from Proverbs: 10:19, 21; 15:22; 17:27 – 28; 18:13; 24:26; 27:5 – 6; 29:11; and 29:20. What does God teach here about words and the tongue?

Love That Lasts

1 CORINTHIANS 13:1 – 13

Jesus predicted that in the last days, because of the increase of wickedness, the love of most will grow cold (Matthew 24:12). Today, an increase of this "cold love" can be found in both the church and the world.

Yet the Bible teaches that God *is* love (1 John 4:16) and that Christians are to be known by their love for one another (John 13:34 – 35).

For this reason, 1 Corinthians 13 is a timely message for us today. Written to a church filled with disunity and pride, this chapter is a beautiful portrait of Christian love. It defines love, explains where it fits in God's agenda for his church, and explores its future in eternity.

WARMING UP

1. Think of a person who is loving. In what specific ways does he or she demonstrate love to others?

DIGGING IN

2.   Read 1 Corinthians 13:1 – 13. What gifts of the Spirit does Paul mention in verses 1 – 3?

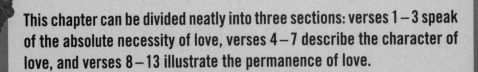

This chapter can be divided neatly into three sections: verses 1 – 3 speak of the absolute necessity of love, verses 4 – 7 describe the character of love, and verses 8 – 13 illustrate the permanence of love.

3.   Powerful and spectacular as these gifts may be, why are they worthless without love?

4.   Why is it easy to fall into the trap of serving others and exercising our spiritual gifts without a heart of love?

When and how has this happened in your service to Jesus and others?

5.   What preventive measures can you take to ensure that love remains your motive in ministry?

6. The world understands a conditional love with strings attached, such as: "I love you if you live up to my expectations," "I love you if you make me feel good," or "I love you if you are rich and beautiful." In verses 4–7 Paul gives God's definition of love. What are the eight characteristics that love *is not*?

"Love keeps no record of wrongs" is translated from a Greek word used in accounting.

7. What are the seven qualities of what love *is*?

How would you briefly define each of love's qualities?

8. Which quality are you most in need of cultivating? Explain.

Verse 7 says, "[Love] always protects, always trusts [is optimistic], always hopes, always perseveres [doesn't quit on people easily]." In what present situation do you need to live out that kind of love?

9.   According to Paul, why is love superior to spiritual gifts (vv. 8 – 13)?

Paul is not arguing for love instead of spiritual gifts. He calls the Corinthian Christians to earnestly seek after spiritual gifts for the sake of building up the body (see 14:1 – 5). Paul understands that without love, spiritual gifts have no usefulness at all.

10.   Why will spiritual gifts, and even knowledge as we understand it, pass away when Jesus Christ appears?

11.   Of the three great virtues — faith, hope, and love — why is love the greatest (v. 13)?

12.   For centuries Christians have noted that this chapter gives us a picture of Jesus. Reread verses 1 – 8, replacing *love* with *Jesus*. What fresh insights and vision does this give you of Jesus?

13. Like Jesus, we are to love others *in spite of* their faults, sins, problems, and so on. Why is that kind of love such an awesome force when unleashed in our personal lives and in the church?

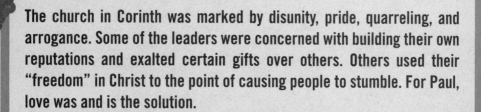

The church in Corinth was marked by disunity, pride, quarreling, and arrogance. Some of the leaders were concerned with building their own reputations and exalted certain gifts over others. Others used their "freedom" in Christ to the point of causing people to stumble. For Paul, love was and is the solution.

14. According to Romans 5:5, "God's love *has been poured out* [past tense] into our hearts through the Holy Spirit, who has been given to us" (italics added). Therefore, we already have his inexhaustible love within us! Describe one situation in which you need this 1 Corinthians 13 love to flow from you to another.

PRAY ABOUT IT

Pray Ephesians 3:14 – 21, asking that you might know the love of Christ and reflect it in all your relationships.

TAKING THE NEXT STEP

Write five thank-you notes to show appreciation and a token of love to others. Then identify five other people who do not love you (see Matthew 5:43 – 48). Ask God for a specific way you can "love" them.

Joy

HOW TO REJOICE IN ANY SITUATION

Phyllis J. LePeau

Introduction

While hunting buffalo in the Dakota Badlands, Theodore Roosevelt spent two weeks in intense heat and driving rain. He got a deep gash in his forehead when his horse reared up unexpectedly. As he crawled on his belly to get a shot at an animal, he accidentally placed his hand on a cactus and received a fistful of spines. That evening, he and his guide were rudely awakened by a cold rain that left them lying in four inches of water. Shivering between sodden blankets, the guide heard Roosevelt exclaim, "By Godfrey, but this is fun!"

Joy is found in the strangest of places — in hospital rooms where patients are weak from surgery, around a dinner table when a husband announces he has been laid off, or in a household where a parent's only companions are little children and the mundane tasks include laundry, cleaning, shopping, and cooking. Although situations like these are seldom "fun," they can be surprising occasions of joy.

How is this possible? The answer is found in two of my favorite songs, "The Joy of the Lord Is My Strength" and "In Thy Presence There Is Fullness of Joy." In my mind they summarize the truth about joy. It is possible to experience joy in the midst of trial, in the midst of weakness, even in the midst of deep pain — because none of these takes us out of God's presence. In fact, they can cause us to go deeper and deeper into his presence. There we find joy. And there we are strengthened by joy.

This may sound simplistic. But I have seen it happen. I have been strengthened by being around those who overflow with joy, whose outlook on the mundane things of life has been transformed by the joy of the Lord. Instead of boredom and complaint, there is life and vibrancy.

And I have seen those in the midst of deep pain, whose world has caved in on them — such as a young man whose wife and unborn child were killed in a car crash — survive on the joy of the Lord. In excruciating agony, he knows "it is well" because the Lord is near. When all of his own physical, emotional, and spiritual strength is drained from his being, the Holy Spirit continues faithfully to produce the fruit of joy.

This section of *Fruit of the Spirit* looks at situations in which joy does not come naturally. The only explanation is that it is a work of the Spirit — joy in trials, joy in weakness, and joy in the gospel (when it involves great personal cost). We will also look at sources of joy — or ways of entering God's presence — joy in the Word, joy in God's discipline, and joy in Christ's rest.

God wants to make us like his Son, who endured the cross "for the joy set before him" (Hebrews 12:2). As you consider what the Scriptures say about the fruit of joy, my prayer is that it will fill your life in unexpected places.

Joy in Trials

JAMES 1:2–12

"Saved alone" was the message that Horatio Spafford received from his wife after the ship sank that was taking her and their four children to England in November 1873. After Spafford reunited with his grieving wife at sea, the boat came near the area where his children had drowned. It is speculated that at that time he wrote the words that vividly described his own grief and faith:

> When sorrows like sea billows roll —
> Whatever my lot
> Thou hast taught me to say,
> It is well, it is well with my soul.

Sorrow is a natural response to trials. But in James 1:2–12 we discover why even in the darkest times of our lives we can say with convincing clarity, "It is well with my soul!"

WARMING UP

1. How does joy differ from happiness?

DIGGING IN

2.   Read James 1:2 – 12. It seems strange that we should "consider it pure joy
     … whenever [we] face trials of many kinds" (v. 2). Why are we to be joyful?

> James not only instructs us to face trials with joy, but with pure joy. In
> the Greek text, the word translated as "pure" is the word *pas*, which is a
> primary word meaning all, every, and whole or thoroughly. James is tell-
> ing us not to "fake it." We should have a joy which is neither contrived
> nor forced as some impossible religious obligation. To the contrary, we
> should have pure, unadulterated, all-encompassing, thorough joy!
>
> Paul A. Cedar, *James, 1, 2 Peter, Jude*, The Communicator's Commentary
>
> [James] most particularly has in mind the trials of being persecuted, the
> trials that come as a consequence of one's faith in Christ.
>
> George M. Stulac, *James*, IVP New Testament Commentary Series

3.   What is perseverance?

     Why is it important in the Christian life?

4. How are perseverance and maturity developed in us by enduring trials (vv. 3 – 4)?

How does our attitude toward these trials affect our growth?

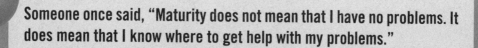

Someone once said, "Maturity does not mean that I have no problems. It does mean that I know where to get help with my problems."

5. How do trials reveal the depth of our character?

What difficult experiences have increased your perseverance and maturity?

6. How might trials expose our need for God's wisdom (v. 5)?

7. According to James, how will God respond to our request for wisdom (v. 5)?

How is this promise a source of joy for you?

8. Under pressure, how does the faithful Christian (vv. 5 – 6) contrast with the person described in verses 6 – 8?

9. In the context of trials and perseverance, why do you think James contrasts rich and poor Christians (vv. 9 – 11)?

10. In what ways do you rely on your possessions for joy?

11. In verse 12 we discover that there is a crown of life for those who persevere in trials. What is a crown of life?

    How can the promise of receiving this crown increase our joy in the midst of trials?

In the New Testament the word *stephanos* denotes a chaplet or a circlet. It is used of Christ's crown of thorns … [but] its more usual use was for the laurel wreath awarded to the victor at the Games or for a festive garland used on occasions of rejoicing.… Sometimes the Christian's crown is here and now, as when Paul thinks of his converts as his crown (Philippians 4:1; 1 Thessalonians 2:19). More usually it is in the hereafter, as the "crown of righteousness, which the Lord, the righteous judge, shall give me at that day" (2 Timothy 4:8).

New Bible Dictionary

PRAY ABOUT IT

Praise God that this passage gives Christians an eternal perspective on trials and suffering. Ask him to make this perspective your perspective as you talk to him about trials and suffering in your life. Pray that you would truly experience joy in trials.

TAKING THE NEXT STEP

Read the following passages of Scripture: Matthew 21:18 – 22; John 1:1 – 13; John 15:18 – 25; John 16:33; Romans 5:1 – 5; 1 Peter 1:3 – 9; and 1 Peter 4:12 – 16. They each contain truth about joy in trials. Then pick one passage, writing down the truths from it and how they relate to your own life and situation. Ask God to integrate the truth of these passages into your heart and mind so that you will live a life of joy in trials.

Joy in Weakness

2 CORINTHIANS 12:1–10

It had been a long time since I had felt this weak and helpless. In tears I shared my distress with my husband, Andy. I was struggling in a couple of relationships. Everything I did seemed to hurt the people I was trying to love. Besides that, I felt I was not growing spiritually. Though my goal for the year was to grow as a person of prayer, my prayer life was at an all-time low. I felt like a miserable failure.

When I was finished, Andy said gently, "You could be in no better place before God. He is much freer to work in us when we are at the end of ourselves."

In 2 Corinthians 12 Paul struggles with a painful weakness but discovers how it can become a source of strength and joy.

WARMING UP

1. When you think of God's power, what comes to mind?

DIGGING IN

2.   Read 2 Corinthians 12:1 – 10. Paul feels forced to "boast" to defend himself against his opponents. How would you summarize his boasting (vv. 1 – 6)?

Evidently [Paul's] opponents had criticized his claim to be an apostle saying that he had not experienced visions and revelations. Paul puts the record straight.

The New Bible Commentary: Revised

3.   Why do you think he refers to "a man in Christ" (v. 2) when speaking about his own experience of being "caught up to the third heaven"?

4.   In spite of his supernatural experiences, Paul wanted people to judge him on his character, not his experiences (v. 6). Why do people's actions and words reveal more about them than their "credentials"?

5.   Why was Paul given a thorn in the flesh (v. 7)?

> The power of Christ is power in weakness; all other power — i.e., power in power — Paul must have found puny in comparison. In this life, only power in weakness is divine and sure to keep divinity where it belongs — with God and not the vessel (2 Corinthians 4:7).
>
> Frederick Dale Bruner, *A Theology of the Holy Spirit*

6. How can our experiences — spiritual and otherwise — lead us to become conceited?

7. Why did God refuse to remove Paul's thorn in spite of his repeated prayers (vv. 8–9)?

8. We usually want God to demonstrate his power by removing our weaknesses. Why is his power more perfectly revealed in the midst of our weaknesses?

9. When have you experienced God's power and sufficient grace in the midst of a painful weakness?

10. What different kinds of experiences qualify as "thorns" in our lives (v. 10)?

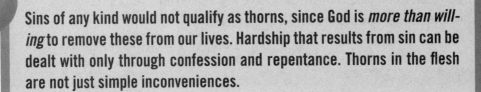

Sins of any kind would not qualify as thorns, since God is *more than willing* to remove these from our lives. Hardship that results from sin can be dealt with only through confession and repentance. Thorns in the flesh are not just simple inconveniences.

11. What thorn is currently causing you pain?

12. What have you learned from this passage that will help you to rejoice in that weakness?

PRAY ABOUT IT

Praise God that weakness has purpose in your life because you belong to the Lord Jesus Christ. Thank him for the ways that you have seen his strength through your weakness.

TAKING THE NEXT STEP

Simon Peter is one of many characters in Scripture who experienced weakness and failure that were turned into strength because of God's power. Look at his life closely through the following passages: Luke 5:1 – 11; 22:31; John 13:1 – 9, 31 – 38; Luke 22:54 – 62; and John 21:15 – 19. Then respond to these questions.

- What do you see of Jesus' vision for Peter?

- What do you see of Peter's love for and loyalty to Jesus?

- In what ways do you see Peter weak and inconsistent?

- Why was it important that Peter's self-confidence and pride be broken?

- How do you identify with Peter?

- What is Jesus' response to Peter's weakness and failure?

- What encouragement do you take as you reflect on 1 Peter 5:8 – 11?

Joy in God's Word

PSALM 119:9–16, 105–112

In her book *The Joy of Discovery*, Oletta Wald writes, "While a student at the former Biblical Seminary in New York, I was taught how to explore the truths of the Bible in a methodical and systematic way.... I found that it was like working a combination lock. When I followed the steps, the Word opened up to me. I felt free. I realized that I was no longer dependent on others to gain insights into Scripture. I had become a discoverer. In a new way, Bible study had become more meaningful and personal. Most of all it was deeply satisfying to know how to discover the truths in God's Word. I had experienced the joy of discovery in Bible study!"

Centuries earlier the psalmist wrote of his own feelings about Scripture. It brought him such joy that he wrote 176 verses describing his response to it. We will look at just a few of those verses in this study as we consider what it means to have joy in God's Word.

WARMING UP

1. If you were to describe your times in Scripture as eating food, what kind of food would it be—blueberry pie, meat and potatoes, green vegetables, whole-grain bread, chicken broth, or what? Explain.

DIGGING IN

2.   Read Psalm 119:9 – 16. How is the psalmist's passion for God's Word evident in these verses?

> Some accuse the psalmist of worshipping the Word rather than the Lord; but it has been well remarked that every reference here to Scripture, without exception, relates it explicitly to its author; indeed every verse from 4 to the end is a prayer or affirmation addressed to Him. This is true piety: a love of God not desiccated by study but refreshed, informed and nourished by it.
>
> Derek Kidner, *Psalms 73 — 150*, Tyndale Old Testament Commentaries

3.   Describe a time when you rejoiced in the Word as one rejoices in great riches.

4.   What are the functions of the Word of God according to this passage?

5.   One of the functions of God's Word is to keep our way pure. What does a pure life depend on according to this passage (vv. 10 – 16)?

6. In what ways have you found it easy to live a pure life according to God's Word?

    How have you found it difficult?

7. Read Psalm 119:105 – 112. Another major function of the Scriptures is guidance (v. 105). In what areas do you rely on God's Word for guidance?

8. What difficulties has the psalmist encountered in following God's Word?

9. In spite of his suffering, how does the psalmist feel about Scripture?

10. How do your responses to Scripture compare to those of the psalmist in both of these passages (vv. 9 – 16, 105 – 112)?

11. The psalmist makes a purposeful choice not to neglect God's Word (v. 16). What choices do you need to make in order for God's Word to play a more vital role in your life?

PRAY ABOUT IT

The psalmist says that the Scriptures are "the joy of my heart." Pray that God will bring joy to your heart as you keep the commitments you have made regarding his Word.

TAKING THE NEXT STEP

Continue your meditation on the Word of God by reflecting on Psalm 119:1 – 8, 17 – 24.

After reading verses 1 – 8, divide a sheet of paper into three columns. In the first column list all the effects of the Word of God in one's life as stated by the passage. In the next column write how you have experienced each, and in the final column, how you would like to grow in experiencing each.

Read verses 17 – 24. List from this passage all that the psalmist asks of God concerning his Word. Ask God to do these things in you. Then, throughout the coming weeks, write down his answers to your requests.

Joy in the Gospel

PHILIPPIANS 1:3 – 26

Debby was captured by guerrilla forces. She was a young missionary nurse, pregnant with her third child. Though her captors were a threat to her life and that of her unborn child, she prayed for them. Even as she feared death, she experienced joy because she saw the gospel at work in the very people who had imprisoned her. In the midst of those awful circumstances, her first concern was that Christ be praised. Debby is a vital testimony of what it means to rejoice in the gospel of Jesus Christ.

We see this same joy in Paul as he desires for the gospel to advance, even at great personal cost.

WARMING UP

1. Have you ever felt joy in the midst of difficult circumstances? If so, why?

DIGGING IN

2.   Read Philippians 1:3 – 26. According to these verses, what reasons might
     Paul have to feel discouraged or depressed (see especially vv. 7, 12 – 14, 22)?

3.   In spite of his personal circumstances, what reasons does Paul give for be-
     ing joyful?

> The church at Philippi was Paul's "joy and crown" (4:1). Of all his
> churches it gave him the least trouble, perhaps no trouble at all, and
> the most satisfaction. So Philippians is a letter of joy, brimming over
> with expressions of gratitude, affection, and love. Philippians is also a
> letter desperately needed by the modern church. It provides a picture
> of a church that takes seriously who she is as partners with Christ in the
> Gospel, who accepts Jesus as Lord and patterns her ministry after Him.
>
> Maxie D. Dunnam, *Galatians, Ephesians, Philippians, Colossians, Philemon*,
> The Communicator's Commentary

4.   Joy usually results when our desires are fulfilled and our values are affirmed.
     What do we learn about Paul's values and desires in this passage?

5. Imagine that you are in Paul's situation—under armed guard, in chains, unable to leave your rented quarters, awaiting trial. How would you feel?

6. What difference would news of the spread of the gospel make in your feelings? (Be honest.) Explain.

7. How do your desires and values compare to Paul's?

Paul's joy often seems baffling to us because we fail to realize how closely our joy is linked to our personal desires and values. If we want to experience Paul's joy, then we must make Jesus Christ and his gospel our greatest desire and our supreme value. Only then will we be able to find joy in the midst of the kind of circumstances Paul faced. As long as we value our personal comfort and pleasure most in life, our joy will always be enslaved to our personal circumstances.

8. Let's look more closely at the gospel in which Paul rejoices. What confidence does he have about the gospel (vv. 6–7)?

How do you respond to the assurance that God will complete the good work he has begun in you?

9.   As God completes his good work in the Philippians and in us, what kind of people does Paul pray we will become (vv. 9 – 11)?

> Love calls for and seeks after knowledge. It is not blind. It does not overlook faults and weaknesses in others, but sees them clearly, looking beyond them to "the heart of things" and continuing to love. Love does not downplay truth, or speak in circles or opaquely to avoid confrontation, but speaks the truth that change and healing may be possible.
>
> Dunnam, *Galatians, Ephesians, Philippians, Colossians, Philemon*

10.   How much does your joy center on the work of the gospel in you and in others?

11.   What substitutes for the gospel do we and our culture gravitate to for sources of joy?

How effective are they in producing joy? Explain.

12. Paul's joy in the gospel was so all-consuming that he proclaimed, "For to me, to live is Christ and to die is gain" (v. 21). What do you need to experience that kind of joyful commitment to Christ?

PRAY ABOUT IT

Thank God for the gospel of Jesus Christ. Confess to him those areas in which your values and desires are not like Paul's. Thank him that he has promised to complete in you the work he began when you became a Christian.

TAKING THE NEXT STEP

Make Paul's prayer for the Philippians your own.

First, make a list of the relationships where you need to love or love more deeply. Ask God to give insight you need about yourself and others in order for your love to grow. Ask him for strength to wrestle with the hard issues of these relationships. Pray that the light of Jesus and the knowledge of his gospel will change how you love others.

Then make a list of situations where you need to be pure and blameless. Ask the Lord to help you differentiate not only between good and evil, but between good and better, and better and best.

Finally, ask God to give you a life of fruitfulness as you participate in the gospel. Ask him to fill you with his joy.

George MacDonald's short story "The Gifts of the Child Christ" describes a little girl who was very sad when she heard Hebrews 12:6, "Whom the Lord loveth he chasteneth" (KJV). She was from a well-to-do family and had suffered very little in life. Since she assumed she had not been disciplined by God, she concluded that he must not love her.

It is, of course, not necessary to draw such a conclusion if God doesn't discipline us at certain times. Yet when God does discipline us, the author of Hebrews gives us several reasons to rejoice.

WARMING UP

1. How do children usually feel about being disciplined by their parents?

DIGGING IN

2.   Read Hebrews 12:1 – 13. The writer of Hebrews compares the Christian life to a race (vv. 1 – 3). What principles for running does he recommend (vv. 1 – 3)?

> Christians ... must be ever watchful of obstructions which, unless removed, will certainly impede their progress. Those hindrances are first likened to "weights" which must be laid aside. The Greek word *ogkon*, weight, in the athletic world of that day was connected with bulk of body or superfluous flesh which had to be removed by right training. But the use of the aorist, *apothemenoi*, lay aside, suggests something which can be thrown off like a garment, which in any race would be a great hindrance.
>
> R. V. W. Tasker, *The Epistle to the Hebrews*, Tyndale New Testament Commentaries

3.   What kinds of "clothing" can hinder us, and what kinds of sins can entangle us as we run?

4.   What does it mean to "fix our eyes on Jesus" (v. 2)?

> In looking to Jesus . . . we are looking to him who is the supreme exponent of faith, the one who, beyond all others, not only set out on the course of faith but also pursued it without wavering to the end. He, accordingly, is uniquely qualified to be the supplier and sustainer of the faith of his followers.
>
> **Philip Edgcumbe Hughes, *A Commentary on the Epistle to the Hebrews***

5. How can focusing on Jesus affect your perseverance in running this race (vv. 2 – 4)?

6. What is encouraging about the fact that the Lord disciplines us (vv. 5 – 11)?

7. What do you think it means to "share in his holiness" (v. 10)?

> The holiness of Christ is both the standard of the Christian character and its guarantee.
>
> ***New Bible Dictionary***

8.   The results of discipline are "a harvest of righteousness and peace" (v. 11). What might this look like in a person's life in concrete, practical ways?

9.   In what sense is God's discipline like physical therapy (vv. 12 – 13)?

Why is it vital for us to cooperate in this therapy?

> Words like *feeble, weak, lame, disabled, healed* all indicate the need for physical therapy. Spiritually speaking, we are lame. God's discipline is like physical therapy designed to strengthen our feeble arms and weak knees. By cooperating with God's therapy, we can be healed. But if we resist because the discipline is too painful or difficult, we can become permanently disabled. Many patients going through physical therapy to recover from some physical injury simply do not do their exercises — and therefore do not improve, at least in a timely fashion. Perseverance is needed through the discipline for its work to be accomplished.

10.   In what ways have you experienced God's discipline in your life?

11.   How do you usually respond to God's discipline?

PRAY ABOUT IT

Praise God for what you have learned about our heavenly Father's discipline in this passage. Pray that he will help you to accept his discipline joyfully. Ask him to produce in you holiness and the fruit of righteousness and peace.

TAKING THE NEXT STEP

Rent the movie *Chariots of Fire*. As you view the movie, note what you see of this passage in it. Consider such things as running the race, the effect of people in the stands cheering the runners on, laying aside weights that hinder and entangle, perseverance and discipline, and losing heart.

Joy in Christ's Rest

MATTHEW 11:28–30

In his hymn "I Heard the Voice of Jesus Say," Horatius Bonar describes Jesus' invitation to the weary and burdened:

> I heard the voice of Jesus say, "Come unto Me and rest:
> Lay down, thou weary one, lay down thy head upon My breast."
> I came to Jesus as I was, weary, and worn, and sad.
> I found in Him a resting-place, and He has made me glad.

There is a part of us that yearns for the rest that Jesus gives. Our lives are full of activity — activity that all too often seems empty and worthless. Quiet and solitude are unheard of. In the midst of our frenzied pace, Jesus continues to gently give the invitation: "Come to me and rest."

WARMING UP

1.   What are some of the deep longings of your heart? For what do you yearn?

DIGGING IN

2.   Read Matthew 11:28 – 30. What invitation does Jesus give in this passage?

3.   What do you think it means to "come to Jesus"?

4.   How easy or difficult is it for you to come to him? Why?

5.   Jesus invites all who are weary and burdened (v. 28). What types of weariness and burdens might he have in mind?

> The common human desire [is] to put the best foot forward and hide from the world our real inward poverty.... There is hardly a man or woman who dares to be just what he or she is without doctoring up the impression. The fear of being found out gnaws like rodents within their hearts.
>
> A. W. Tozer, *The Pursuit of God*

6.   To what extent do you identify with the weary and burdened? Explain.

7.   What is a yoke (v. 29), and what does it do?

What does it mean, therefore, to take Christ's yoke upon us?

8.   What promises does Jesus make to those who respond to his invitation?

> Rest in verses 28 and 29 ... would perhaps be more accurately, and less misleadingly, translated "relief." Certainly Jesus does not promise His disciples a life of inactivity or repose, nor freedom from sorrow and struggle, but He does assure them that, if they keep close to Him, they will find relief from such crushing burdens as crippling anxiety, the sense of frustration and futility, and the misery of a sin-laden conscience.
>
> R. T. France, *Matthew: An Introduction and Commentary*, Tyndale New Testament Commentaries

9.   What would it mean to you to find "rest for your soul"?

How would finding rest for your soul bring you joy?

10. How does it help you to know that Christ's yoke is easy and his burden is light (v. 30)?

The gracious invitation ... is recorded only by Matthew. It is addressed in the first instance to those upon whose backs the Pharisees were laying heavy burdens by demanding meticulous obedience not only to the law itself but to their own intricate elaborations of it. Every law-abiding person is of necessity under a yoke, and the expression "the yoke of the law" was commonplace in Judaism (cf. Acts 15:10). Jesus the Messiah also calls His disciples to accept a "yoke," but how different is His yoke! In the first place it is not really obedience to any external law at all, for it is first and foremost loyalty to a Person, which enables the disciple to do gladly, and therefore easily, and without feeling that he is struggling under a heavy burden, what that Person would have him to do.... Where a relationship exists between a disciple and Himself (His) yoke is easy and (His) burden is light. Moreover, the way of life that He desires His disciples to follow is His own life.

France, *Matthew: An Introduction and Commentary*

11. Jesus describes himself as "gentle and humble in heart" (v. 29). How do these qualities increase your desire to come to him and learn from him?

12. How does the rest Jesus promises in this passage speak to the yearnings and longings of your heart?

PRAY ABOUT IT

Ask God to reveal to you specific ways you can respond to Jesus' invitation to rest. Thank him for the joy we have when we experience Christ's rest.

TAKING THE NEXT STEP

As you respond to Jesus' invitation to come to him, reflect on Philippians 2:5 – 11. Ask Jesus to give you the rest that comes from making his mind and attitude your own. Ask him to deliver you from competition, pretense, and arrogance. Talk to him about the desire you have to freely serve others with joy. Praise him for who he is and because God has given him a name that is above every name.

Peace

OVERCOMING ANXIETY
AND CONFLICT

Jack Kuhatschek

Introduction

I am afraid of heights. I have been known to crawl on my hands and knees to the edge of a high balcony in order to look down. Imagine, then, how I felt when a camp director told me I had to rappel down the side of a steep cliff. "Everyone does it," he said matter-of-factly. "It's part of our program."

With sweaty palms and pounding heart, I eased backward off the edge of the cliff, supported by a rope and a safety line. In order to walk down the face of the cliff, I was told to keep my body perpendicular to the cliff. Every nerve and fiber screamed at me to straighten up, to get in a vertical, not a horizontal position. Yet those who did so lost their footing and were left dangling high above the ground. Only by fighting my natural urges, and by trusting the ropes and those who held them, did I manage to make it safely to the bottom. What a relief!

That fearful experience of rappelling has become a parable of faith to me. There have been many times in my life when God has asked me to ease over the edge of a cliff, to trust him for something that seemed unsafe and frightening. The primary difference, of course, is that both the safety rope and the person at the top of the cliff are invisible — while the cliff and its dangers are in plain sight!

In order to fight my natural urges and to obey what God was calling me to do, I have had to go to Scripture again and again. I have read and reread those passages that assure me of God's presence and support. God is the one who holds the rope, they tell me, and he will never let me fall.

This section of *Fruit of the Spirit* explores six of those passages — the ones that have been most helpful to me during times of anxiety and conflict. The peace they offer is not a permanent possession. Rather, it is experienced afresh with each new challenge. My prayer is that by reading and meditating on them, you will grow in your trust of "the God who holds in his hand your life and all your ways" (Daniel 5:23).

Coping with Anxiety

PHILIPPIANS 4:4–9

Garrison Keillor, author of *Lake Wobegon Days*, writes that his greatest fear as a child was of getting his tongue stuck on a frozen pump handle. The older boys told him that if he touched his tongue to a pump handle, the only way to get him loose would be to rip his tongue right out of his mouth or else put a tent over him until spring.

We all suffer from fears and anxieties of various sorts. Yet if we fail to deal with our anxieties, they can cripple and immobilize us. In Philippians 4, Paul gives us a prescription for inner peace.

WARMING UP

1. What sorts of things make you feel anxious?

DIGGING IN

2. Read Philippians 4:4–9. Paul begins by telling us repeatedly to "rejoice in the Lord always" (v. 4). What does it mean to rejoice in the Lord?

Why is this kind of rejoicing possible in any circumstances?

We are to rejoice in the *Lord*, not necessarily in the circumstances that surround us. Christians in Paul's day faced persecutions and difficulties of various sorts. Paul himself was writing as a prisoner in Rome.

3. Why is prayer (v. 6) our first and best defense against anxiety?

4. Why is it important to be thankful in the midst of our requests?

Paul uses several key words in verse 6: "Prayer" denotes the petitioner's attitude of mind as worshipful. "Petition" denotes prayers as expressions of need. "Thanksgiving" should accompany all Christian praying, as the supplicant acknowledges that whatever God sends is for his good. It may also include remembrance of previous blessings. "Requests" refers to the things asked for.

Homer A. Kent Jr., *Philippians*, The Expositor's Bible Commentary

5. Paul compares the peace of God to a sentry guarding our hearts and minds from anxiety (v. 7). Why do you think Paul adds that God's peace "transcends all understanding"?

God's peace is not dependent on our figuring out a solution to what bothers us, nor is it dependent on our understanding how God will solve our problem. In fact, his help is often beyond our comprehension.

6. Anxious people can become obsessed with negative thinking. How can focusing on the good things in verse 8 free us from the grip of anxiety?

7. Give specific examples of the kinds of good things you might think about to combat anxiety.

8. According to verse 9, what is our third defense against anxiety?

9. How can observing the godly example of others and putting into practice what we see bring greater peace to our lives?

10. What anxious thoughts have troubled you recently?

PRAY ABOUT IT

Take time now to bring your anxieties to God in prayer. Remember to thank him for what he has already done and for what he will do for you in the future.

TAKING THE NEXT STEP

During anxious times, the psalmist encourages us to remember what God has done for us in the past (see Psalms 77, 105, 143). Read one or more of these psalms. Then take time to remember and record some of the ways God has helped, strengthened, or delivered you in the past. Allow his faithfulness to fill your mind and heart in the present.

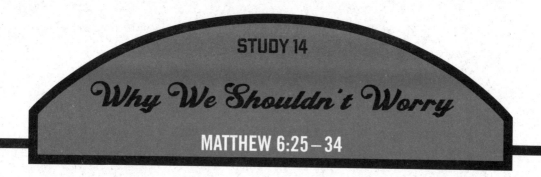

Why We Shouldn't Worry

MATTHEW 6:25 – 34

"Don't worry. Be happy." These words of a popular 1980s song are fun to sing, but they provide no real help to the worrier. Telling an anxious person not to worry is like telling a cold, hungry person to be warmed and filled. Why shouldn't we worry when we face the daily pressure of providing food and clothing for ourselves and our families?

In Matthew 6:25 – 34 Jesus does more than simply telling us not to worry. He tells us why we shouldn't worry.

WARMING UP

1. What are some common reasons why people worry?

DIGGING IN

2. Read Matthew 6:25 – 34. What, specifically, does Jesus tell us not to worry about (vv. 25, 28, 31 – 32)?

Which of these, if any, causes the greatest anxiety in your life? Why?

3.   In what sense is life more important than food, and the body more important than clothes (v. 25)?

4.   According to Jesus, how can we be confident that the Father will feed us and clothe us (vv. 26 – 30)?

5.   Many people, including some Christians, have little food to eat and are dressed much worse than Solomon, not to mention the lilies. How, then, are we to understand Christ's assurances about food and clothes?

Only when we have been liberated from anxiety about our own food and clothes — a liberation devoutly to be desired in Western Christendom — will we give necessary attention to the food and clothing of the Poor World around us. Thus Jesus' text is not antisocial; it is antiselfish. It does not tell us to be unanxious about others' food, but to be unanxious about our own. It does not preach indifference to society; it preaches a rejection of Christians' unbelieving anxiety about themselves and their circumscribed obsessions. Anxious care is the denial of God; it is acting as if we are alone in the world and that either there is no God or that he does not care.

Frederick Dale Bruner, *The Christbook*

6.   In what ways have you seen God provide for your basic needs?

7.   According to verse 27, why is it futile to worry?

     If worry is a waste of time and energy, then why do you think it is such a popular pastime?

8.   In what sense are we acting like pagans when we fret about food or clothing (vv. 31 – 32)?

     When you are anxious, how does it help you to know that your heavenly Father knows your needs (v. 32)?

9.   In contrast to pagan pursuits, what does it mean to "seek first his kingdom and his righteousness" (v. 33)?

This verse makes it clear that Jesus' disciples are not simply to *refrain* from the *pursuit* of temporal things as their primary goal in order to differentiate themselves from pagans. Instead, they are to *replace* such pursuits with goals of far greater significance.

D. A. Carson, *Matthew*, The Expositor's Bible Commentary

In the end, just as there are only two kinds of piety, the self-centered and the God-centered, so there are only two kinds of ambition: one can be ambitious either for oneself or for God. There is no third alternative.

John Stott, *The Message of the Sermon on the Mount*

10. According to Jesus, why is it best to take one day at a time (v. 34)?

PRAY ABOUT IT

Thank the Father for the way he cares and provides for our basic needs. Ask him to help you to act less like a pagan worrier and more like a kingdom seeker.

TAKING THE NEXT STEP

When we worry about the future, we are fighting with "ghosts" — things that do not exist and which may never exist. Instead of expending energy and anxiety on these phantoms, ask God to give you grace for what you are facing today and today only. Leave the unknown future in his hands.

Finding Peace in God's Presence
PSALM 46

The eye of a hurricane is a remarkable place. Fierce, destructive winds spiral around it at terrifying speeds. Torrential rains encircle it, bringing floods and pounding waves. But within the eye itself, everything is calm and peaceful — a quiet refuge in the midst of the storm.

Psalm 46 describes such a place, a spiritual haven from the destructive forces that sometimes surround us.

WARMING UP

1. What frightens you most about such natural forces as hurricanes, torna-does, and earthquakes?

DIGGING IN

2. Read Psalm 46. What portrait of God emerges from verse 1?

Martin Luther's battle-hymn, *Ein' feste Burg*, took its starting-point from this psalm, catching its indomitable spirit but striking out in new directions.... [The psalm's] robust, defiant tone suggests that it was composed at a time of crisis, which makes the confession of faith doubly impressive.

Derek Kidner, *Psalms 1 – 72*, Tyndale Old Testament Commentaries

3.   As you read verses 2 – 3, what images come to mind?

4.   What kinds of personal events can make us feel like the world is falling apart around us?

5.   How does the scene described in verses 4 – 5 contrast with the previous scene?

What aspects of the city of God seem most inviting to you?

The "city of God" (v. 4) refers primarily to Jerusalem, the earthly dwelling place of God at the time this psalm was written. Although Jerusalem had no river like the cities of Thebes, Damascus, Babylon, and Nineveh, God himself was their river, providing them with constant spiritual refreshment even in the midst of a crisis. Later biblical authors pick up this theme and describe the river flowing through the heavenly Jerusalem (see Revelation 22:1–2). In a personal sense, however, the promises of the psalm are not tied to an earthly or heavenly location but assure us of God's presence with his people at all times and places. "Break of day" (v. 5) describes the time when armies normally attacked a city.

6.   Verses 7 and 11 describe God as our fortress. What purposes does a fortress serve in wartime?

How is it reassuring to know that our fortress is the Lord Almighty?

Old Testament battle stories have as one of their staples fortresses — thick-walled cities, often on high mountains, meant to be impenetrable and intimidating to enemies. Yet of the approximately thirty-five references to fortresses in English Bibles, most are metaphoric pictures of God and his acts of salvation . . . [he is] the source of hope and salvation that no enemy — physical or spiritual — can ever threaten.

The Dictionary of Biblical Imagery

7. Verses 6–10 also describe the Lord as a warrior. What effect does he have on the battles among nations?

8. What active role does the Lord take in the battles we face in life (see, for example, Romans 8:26–27; 1 Corinthians 10:13; 2 Corinthians 1:3–11; Ephesians 6:10–18)?

9. In our active, take-charge culture, the command to "be still" (Psalm 46:10) seems completely out of place. What does it mean to be still before God?

   How can our obedience to this command bring about a more exalted view of God?

PRAY ABOUT IT

Think of the battles you are currently facing. How can you allow the Lord to be both your fortress and your warrior in those battles? Bring those battles to him in prayer.

TAKING THE NEXT STEP

Find a quiet place where you can be alone with God. It can be a favorite room in your house, a coffee shop, a park, or a garden. Bring your Bible with you and spend time reading and meditating on Psalm 46. Imagine yourself sitting by one of the streams that brings joy to the city of God, the holy place where the Most High dwells. Praise God for his peace and protection.

Feeling Safe in God's Care

PSALM 91

In 1956 Jim Elliot and four other missionaries were killed by the Auca Indians. Later, his widow, Elisabeth, wrote about the events leading up to Jim's death in a book entitled *Shadow of the Almighty*. The title was taken from Psalm 91, which, ironically, promises God's protection for those who trust in him. The sweeping promises of the psalm force us to wrestle with a nagging question: How can we feel safe in God's care in a world where bad things happen to good people?

WARMING UP

1. When you were a child, what made you feel safe and secure?

DIGGING IN

2. Read Psalm 91. What images does the psalmist use to describe God's protective care?

The word *shelter* (v. 1) may be a reference to the temple. However, it is God's shelter, a place of refuge. In addition to the images, four divine names are used in the psalm: *Most High*, *Almighty*, *Lord*, and *my God*.

3. How does each image affect your feeling of safety?

4. What types of danger are mentioned in the psalm?

   What modern-day counterparts might we face?

5. Is the psalmist really promising that nothing bad will happen to those who trust in God? Explain.

Clearly, the psalmist is not promising freedom from all adversity, for he mentions terrors, arrows, pestilence, plague, battles, disasters, snakes, and so on. Yet if this psalm were our only guide, it would seem to promise that none of these things will hurt us. However, this psalm is *not* our only guide. Other passages of Scripture must also be considered, including those that describe the sufferings of Christ. When taken together, the most that can be said is that nothing harmful will happen to us unless the Lord allows it.

6. In Luke 4:10 – 11 Satan applies the promise of this psalm to Jesus. Yet how do Christ's own experiences cause us to examine the type of protection God offers?

7. What does it mean to make the Most High our "dwelling" and "refuge" (Psalm 46:9)?

8. Verses 9 – 13 speak of God's commanding his angels to guard us. How do you respond to the idea that you have guardian angels?

Have you ever sensed their presence in the midst of danger? Explain.

9.   In verses 14–16 the psalmist becomes silent and God speaks. Read these
     verses to yourself, substituting your name for the pronouns *he* and *him.*

     How does it make you feel to have the Lord speak to you in that way?

10. What current circumstances make you feel unsafe or vulnerable?

     How does this psalm help you to feel safer in God's care?

PRAY ABOUT IT

Bring your current circumstances to the Lord in prayer. Thank him for being your
dwelling and refuge.

TAKING THE NEXT STEP

The psalmist describes the Lord as a refuge, fortress, mother bird, shield, rampart, and dwelling. Which of these images make you feel protected and safe? Meditate on those images, imagining yourself under God's protection. Since these images are not fiction but reality, how should your life be different this week and beyond … at work, financially, in your family, as you face the future?

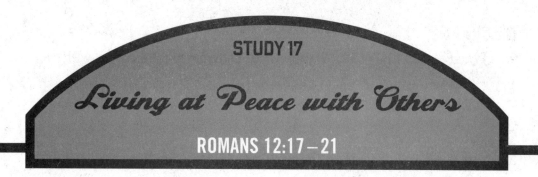

Living at Peace with Others

ROMANS 12:17 – 21

One day someone dumped a large load of garbage into the creek behind the house of a friend of mine. As my friend was cleaning up the soggy mess, he noticed an envelope with a man's name and address on it. He promptly loaded up the garbage and drove to the man's house. Just as the man was coming out his front door, my friend dumped the entire pile of garbage into his front yard. The man stood there dumbfounded as my friend drove away laughing.

Was my friend right or wrong in his action? Romans 12:17 – 21 gives us guidelines for responding to those who mistreat us.

WARMING UP

1.   How would you have responded if someone had dumped a load of garbage in your yard? Why?

DIGGING IN

2. Read Romans 12:17 – 21. Why are we often tempted to repay evil with evil?

3. Give examples of some of the ways people and countries repay evil with evil.

    How does revenge frequently make things worse rather than better?

4. Paul commands us to live at peace with everyone — with two qualifications: "if it is possible" and "as far as it depends on you" (v. 18). Why are these qualifications important?

> **There may be times when peace is not possible, in spite of our best efforts and intentions.**

5. Why do you think God forbids us to take revenge, reserving vengeance for himself (v. 19; see also Deuteronomy 32:35)?

> There is no suggestion that the wrath of God will be visited upon the wrongdoer immediately. On the contrary, that wrath is the last resort, for in the immediate future lies the possibility that the one who has perpetrated the wrong will have a change of heart and will be convicted of his sin and won over by the refusal of the Christian to retaliate (v. 20).
>
> Everett F. Harrison, *Romans*, The Expositor's Bible Commentary

6.   How can the promise of God's wrath help restrain our desire for revenge?

7.   In verse 20 Paul quotes Proverbs 25:21 – 22. What is radical about the advice of this proverb?

> Providing for an enemy's hunger and thirst is similar to the actions Jesus requires of us in response to an enemy: turning the other cheek, giving our shirts to those who ask for our coats, and giving to those who beg from us (Luke 6:29 – 30).
>
> Douglas Moo, *Romans*, The NIV Application Commentary

8.   What do you think it means to "heap burning coals" on our enemy's head (v. 20; see also Proverbs 25:21 – 22)?

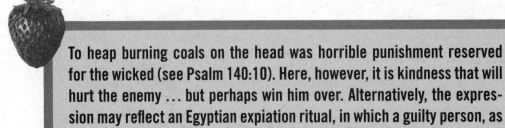

To heap burning coals on the head was horrible punishment reserved for the wicked (see Psalm 140:10). Here, however, it is kindness that will hurt the enemy ... but perhaps win him over. Alternatively, the expression may reflect an Egyptian expiation ritual, in which a guilty person, as a sign of his repentance, carried a basin of glowing coals on his head. The meaning here, then, would be that in returning good for evil and so being kind to your enemy, you may cause him to repent or change.

The NIV Study Bible, note on Proverbs 25:22

9.   In addition to giving food and water to our enemy, what are some other ways we might overcome evil with good (v. 21)?

10.   Think of someone who has recently mistreated you. What might you do to promote peace with that person?

PRAY ABOUT IT

Spend time now praying for the person who has mistreated you, asking God to help you overcome evil with good.

TAKING THE NEXT STEP

Make a genuine effort this week to do something kind and gracious to the person who has mistreated you. Let it be a first step in living at peace with him or her.

Ruth ⇒ pregnancy of HA

Li → stable job

Hilary → Faith

Bonnie alken → good jobs

Christ, Our Peace

EPHESIANS 2:11—22

In *The Adventures of Huckleberry Finn*, Huck visits Tom's Aunt Sally. She immediately begins probing him about why he arrived so late:

"We been expecting you a couple of days and more. What kep' you?—boat get aground?"

"Yes'm ... but it warn't the grounding—that didn't keep us back but a little. We blowed out a cylinder head."

"Good gracious! Anybody hurt?"

"No'm. Killed a nigger."

Racial prejudice has always plagued humanity. But our hostility runs deeper than race. National pride, ethnic superiority, class distinctions, religious and cultural bigotry—each one drives a wedge between us and our neighbor. In Ephesians 2 Paul explains how Christ has demolished the barriers that divide us.

WARMING UP

1. Why do you think people often feel a need to distinguish between "us" and "them"?

DIGGING IN

2.   Read Ephesians 2:11 – 22. The Jews called the Gentiles "uncircumcised" (v. 11) and even referred to them as "dogs" (Matthew 15:26). What labels do people today apply to those who are different from them?

What is wrong with such labels?

3.   In what ways were the Gentiles truly separated from the Jews (Ephesians 2:12)?

The apostle urges the Ephesians to recollect what they once were in their heathen state. Four successive phrases depict their debits as compared with those of the Jews (cf. Romans 9:4, 5). In the first place, they were without or apart (NIV, "separate") from Christ. They had no expectation of a Messiah to light up their darkness. They knew nothing at all about him. They had no rights of citizenship (*politea*) in his kingdom. They were cut off from any such privilege by reason of their birth…. They lived in a world devoid of hope (1 Thessalonians 4:13). They were, moreover, "without God" (*atheoi*). This does not imply that they were forsaken by God, but that, since they were ignorant of him (Galatians 4:8), they did not believe in him.

A. Skevington Wood, *Ephesians*, The Expositor's Bible Commentary

4.   In what ways are non-Christians today truly separated from Christians?

5.   What did Christ do to end the hostility and separation between Jews and Gentiles (vv. 13 – 18)?

Paul describes the separation between Jews and Gentiles as a "barrier" and as a "dividing wall of hostility" (v. 14). [The Jewish historian] Josephus used each of these terms separately with reference to the balustrade in the Jerusalem temple separating the court of the Gentiles from the temple proper. On it was an inscription that read: "No foreigner may enter within the barricade which surrounds the sanctuary and enclosure. Anyone who is caught doing so will have himself to blame for his ensuing death." When Jerusalem fell in AD 70, this partition was demolished along with the temple itself. But Paul saw it as already destroyed by Christ at the cross.

Wood, *Ephesians*

6.   Why does Christ's death destroy all the racial, ethnic, and social distinctions that often separate us from others?

7.   What do we now have in common with everyone who is "in Christ" — even with those whom we formerly despised (vv. 14 – 22)?

8.   In what sense, if any, does Christ bring peace between us and those who do not yet know him?

9.   If we are truly one in Christ with all who know him, then why are so many churches divided on the basis of race, ethnic origin, and social status?

10.   What might we do to encourage greater diversity in our churches?

11.   What might you do in your family to encourage greater acceptance of those who are different?

PRAY ABOUT IT

Think of one way in which prejudice is still a problem for you. Ask God to allow the fruit of peace to overcome that prejudice.

TAKING THE NEXT STEP

What ethnic groups or minorities in your area are looked down on or despised? Take a piece of paper and divide it into two columns. In the left column make a list of some of the reasons for this prejudice. In the right column record what Christ has done to overcome each item on your list. How should that reality affect your relationship with these people?

Patience

THE BENEFITS
OF WAITING

Stephen Eyre

Introduction

"Lord, I want patience, and I want it right now!" It is easier to joke about patience than to become patient. You can tell that God is growing patience in you, not when you are patient, but when you run into frustrating experiences; when others fail to meet your expectations; when people you depend on let you down; when the things you depend on keep breaking. Most of all, you know you are learning patience when you call out to the Lord for help, and he seems to be on vacation.

I am not an expert on patience; it doesn't come naturally to me. I am constantly aware that there is more to do than there is time to do it. Frequently, a sense of urgency pushes me from the inside.

There are lots of reasons for this inward push: my desire to feel important and productive, and the perceived expectations of family and friends to get things done. Even the commercials on television tell me to hurry if I am to take advantage of the best deal available "today only."

God is not pleased with this sense of hurry. As a result, my life with him has included a lengthy term of schooling in a different way of living. When I say, "quick," God seems to say, "slow." When I say, "now," God seems to say, "later."

In puzzling through these frustrating interactions with God, I have come to see that waiting, and the patience it requires, occupies a central role in Scripture in shaping God's people. God called Abraham and promised him a whole nation of children. Yet during his life Abraham had only one covenanted son, and he had to wait over twenty-five years for him to be born. Along the way, Abraham had some very wonderful and very painful times with God.

God called David to be the king of Israel. But before David ascended to the throne, he had to live as a fugitive in the desert for ten years while Saul chased him. Even a cursory look at the book of Psalms reveals that David did not enjoy those years. Yet God thought they were important for David and used them to shape David's character.

Learning to wait patiently on God is worth it. The benefits include the ability to influence others in godliness, the certainty of God's blessings, a deeper knowledge of Scripture, a growing patience with and forgiveness of others, and a certain hope to sustain us even in the darkest times.

In this section of *Fruit of the Spirit* we will look at the benefits of patience, the blessings of perseverance, the virtue of slowness, patience and forgiveness, waiting for the Lord, and waiting until the end. As you work through each of these six studies, my prayer is that you will begin to see the fruit of patience ripening in your life.

The Benefits of Patience

SELECTED PROVERBS

"Stop it!"

"No!"

"You are going to break Dad's computer!"

"It's my turn!"

The game of computer Monopoly comes to an abrupt halt. My youngest son stomps out of the study and runs upstairs to his room. My two older sons walk away, exasperated. So much for a quiet Sunday afternoon.

With a little more patience the game could have gone on. But the boys were tired, and it was a hot afternoon. Patience on such days is not in great supply.

For most of us, more is at stake during frustrating times than a children's game. Yet it is in the trying times, when we seem least inclined to be patient, that we need it the most. We can be encouraged to grow in patience if we look at its benefits in the book of Proverbs.

WARMING UP

1.   Take a patience inventory. At what times and in what circumstances do you tend to be impatient?

DIGGING IN

2.   Read the following verses from the book of Proverbs: 14:29; 15:18; 16:32; 19:11; and 25:15. How would you summarize the qualities of a patient person?

3.   What contrasts are drawn between a patient and an impatient person?

4.   According to Proverbs 15:18, how does patience/impatience affect our relationships with others?

How have you seen patience/impatience affect relationships in your life?

5. Reread Proverbs 16:32. Why do you think a patient person is better than a warrior or one who takes a city?

6. How could patience be a great asset in your (choose one) workplace, classroom, home?

7. How does patience — or the lack of it — reveal whether a person is wise or foolish (14:29; 19:11)?

8. Think of a person you know who is very patient. In what other ways does that person seem wise?

9. According to Proverbs 15:18 and 25:15, how does patience or impatience affect the impact of our speech?

10. Look at Proverbs 16:32 and 25:15. What is the difference between patience and passiveness?

What is the difference between patience and powerlessness?

> We may think of a patient person as passive and powerless. Nothing could be further from the truth. Our Lord is the best illustration of true patience. He was neither passive nor powerless.

11.   What changes do you need to make in the way you act and think in order to become more patient?

PRAY ABOUT IT

Based on this study, perhaps we could say that patience requires faith and leads to wisdom. Ask God to bless you with a faith that trusts and leads you to wisdom.

TAKING THE NEXT STEP

How we face our anger is directly related to our patience. This week, keep a daily journal of every occasion you have to be angry. Before you go to bed, offer your anger and accompanying frustrations to the Lord. At the end of the week, reflect on how facing your anger affected your patience.

At one point in my ministry I was not seeing much fruit. At least not to my satisfaction. I struggled with such questions as, Why aren't there more converts? Why aren't there more people in Bible studies? And why aren't there more growing Christians?

At such times I was tempted to ponder if I was in the wrong profession. Maybe I ought to give up and get a "real" job. Then I would remind myself that I minister not for results, but because I am called.

Perhaps you have similar frustrations about some aspect of your Christian experience. Perhaps things haven't turned out the way you thought they would. Sometimes you wonder whether it would be easier just to give up and go with the flow of the world around you.

The Christian life has been described as "a long obedience in the same direction." We must keep on believing, day in and day out, for years. Yet we can keep going only if we develop an important part of patience — perseverance. James 5 helps us understand that vital quality.

WARMING UP

1.   In what area of life have you been tempted to "give up"?

DIGGING IN

2.   Read James 5:7 – 12. What three examples of perseverance does James give?

3.   What can the farmer teach us about the value of patience (v. 7)?

Rain is scarce in Israel and comes only in the autumn and spring. If a drought comes during those seasons, the farmers' crops are wiped out for the year.

4.   What might cause us to grumble against each other (v. 9) as we wait for the Lord's return?

5.   What happens to fellowship among believers when they grumble against each other?

6.   How does the warning that "the Judge is standing at the door" (v. 9) address the problem of grumbling?

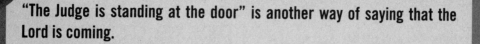

"The Judge is standing at the door" is another way of saying that the Lord is coming.

7. Three times in verses 7–9 James refers to the Lord's coming. Why does James see it as so important for perseverance?

How does the Lord's return affect your perspective on life?

8. The prophets (v. 10) are an example of patience in suffering, especially since few ever saw any results from their ministry. How do you think they could keep going when God's people rejected their message?

9. Job is also an illustration of patience (v. 11). When he faced severe suffering, his friends weren't good comforters. How can friends sometimes increase the pain of suffering?

How can friends give us strength to persevere in suffering?

10. Another reason to be patient is because of the Lord's compassion and mercy (v. 11). How can these aspects of the Lord's character give you strength to keep going?

11. James gives a severe warning against swearing—taking an oath to guarantee the truth of what you say (v. 12). Why does swearing bring God's condemnation (v. 12; see also Matthew 5:33–37)?

During the time at which James was writing, oaths and swearing had developed into a very intricate system of calling on God and binding commitments to God if he chose to come to the aid of the oath maker. Incredible distinctions proliferated under such an approach. Swearing by heaven and earth was not binding, nor was swearing *by* Jerusalem, though swearing *toward* Jerusalem was.... Many groups (e.g., Anabaptists, Jehovah's Witnesses) have understood these verses absolutely literally and have therefore refused even to take court oaths. Their zeal to conform to Scripture is commendable, but they have probably not interpreted the text very well.... The contextual purpose of this passage is to stress the true direction in which the Old Testament points—the importance of truthfulness. Where oaths are not being used evasively and truthfulness is not being threatened, it is not immediately obvious that they require such unqualified abolition.

D. A. Carson, *Matthew*, The Expositor's Bible Commentary

12. Look again at the entire passage. Summarize why perseverance is important for us as Christians.

PRAY ABOUT IT

Ask the Lord to give you the faith and spiritual strength to persevere in the challenges and difficulties you face.

TAKING THE NEXT STEP

Perseverance is intimately tied to disappointments. Keep a record of things that disappoint you. Observe your first response to each disappointment. After writing down that first response, lift your disappointment to the Lord in prayer, and then notice how your attitude toward it is affected.

The Virtue of Slowness

Occasionally a driver would swerve around me, casting looks of impatient disgust and a few choice words. I felt bad, but there was little I could do.

We were on a family vacation in a part of the world we had never been to before. Since I didn't know my way around, it was slow going. Looking at road signs and pondering maps takes time. Some drivers behind me were not appreciative.

Living the Christian life can be slow going as well. In fact, the Christian life *should* be slow going. Our initial responses are not always godly ones, and we need to carefully consider our actions and seek the Lord's guidance.

WARMING UP

1. How do you respond when others around you don't seem to know what they are doing and get in your way?

DIGGING IN

2.   Read James 1:19–27. The three paragraphs included in these verses are very closely connected, yet don't necessarily appear to be at first glance. To help you get an overview of the passage, give a brief title to each one (vv. 19–21, 22–25, 26–27).

James addresses speaking, righteous living, and turning from the world in the first paragraph and picks up on those same issues in the third as well. The middle paragraph is the key and addresses all those issues.

3.   In verse 19, being slow to speak and slow to anger is an important part of a righteous life. How do you think "quick listening" can slow us down and help us to live righteously?

4.   Recall a time when you spoke too quickly. Was it related to anger?

What consequences did it have in your life?

5. Hasty talk and anger are often expressions of worldliness still in our hearts. How can we get rid of moral filth and evil (v. 21)?

The Greek word for "moral filth" can also be translated as "impurity." It means having mixed motives, some from the world and some from Scripture. James calls us to get rid of our worldly impurities.

6. Getting rid of moral filth and evil requires that we accept the Word (v. 21). If the Word is already implanted in us, why do we need to humbly accept it?

7. "Slow" action doesn't mean no action. What is the proper approach to God's Word according to verses 22 – 25?

8. Self-identity is a major issue in counseling today. How can Scripture affect our sense of identity (vv. 23 – 25)?

9.   In our culture there is a tendency to think of laws as inhibiting, yet James describes Scripture as the perfect law that gives freedom (v. 25). How can God's law give freedom?

The idea of law is very biblical but not very modern. In a relativistic age, law is seen as an infringement of personal rights and a restriction of personal self-realization. In the Old Testament the Law was seen as a gift from God to guide us in the right and healthy way of life (see Psalm 119).

10.   Twice James warns against self-deception (vv. 22, 26). How would you define self-deception?

We can deceive ourselves by forgetfulness, listening without doing, or undisciplined talking. Which kind of deception are you most prone to?

James used two words for *deception*. The one in verse 22 means to "talk around" the truth. The one in verse 26 means to "walk around" the truth. He also implies a third way of deception, forgetfulness. We simply forget to do the truth. Self-deception is very dangerous because we are usually blind to our deception. James exposes our blindness by calling us to look at our actions.

11. Read verses 26 – 27. Which of the three marks of godly religious behavior mentioned here do you find in your life?

What can you do about the areas where you are weakest?

PRAY ABOUT IT

Ask God to show you ways to slow down the pace of your life so that you can listen properly to God's Word as he guides you.

TAKING THE NEXT STEP

Our first response is not always the best response. Perhaps we could say that our first response is the "natural" response, while our second response could be a "supernatural" response — the response we would give if we took time to prayerfully reflect before we spoke or acted. Sometime in the evening each day during the next week, set aside a few moments to think back over your day. Check to see how many "first responses" determined your behavior as opposed to the number of "second responses" you made.

Patience and Forgiveness

MATTHEW 18:15—35

A quiet disagreement developed between Mike and me. And it grew.

I was never sure what it was about. I approached him about it once, but he said everything was fine, no problems. So I let it go, and it festered under the surface, occasionally breaking into subtle power struggles in our leadership meetings.

I should have approached him again, but I moved before I got around to it. I was glad to let it go — until I got a letter from a mutual friend. He called me to account, saying that the division between Mike and me was not pleasing to God. He still sensed, even over the thousands of miles, an underlying hostility on both sides. He was right.

So I wrote a letter to Mike, and he wrote back. "Yes," he said, "I am angry." At that point we began the slow and painful process of reconciliation.

In Matthew 18 Jesus tells us that good relationships require work, a special kind of determination, patience, and mercy.

WARMING UP

1.   When someone offends you, how do you tend to respond?

DIGGING IN

2.   Read Matthew 18:15–20. When a Christian sins against us, Jesus tells us to "go and point out their fault" (v. 15). Why not just avoid the person who offended us?

Jesus commands us to love one another: "A new command I give you: Love one another. As I have loved you, so you must love one another" (John 13:34). This command requires us to embrace others who follow Jesus, even if it is uncomfortable.

3.   Why do we sometimes want to avoid the process of confrontation and reconciliation?

4.   Initially, why is it important to talk privately with the person, keeping the matter "just between the two of you" (v. 15)?

5.   If the person will not listen to you, what is the benefit of taking one or two others with you (v. 16)?

Following Christ is not a solitary act; we are joined with each other. When we go with others, they can help us and the other person to see things from a different angle. They may even discover areas where we need to apologize.

Why can taking others also be threatening?

Telling people they owe us an apology can be threatening—for us as well as for them. For one thing, confrontation doesn't always bring a positive response on the other person's part. For another, we can appear to be self-righteous and snobbish to the other person. (Which may, in fact, be true.)

6.   Why do you think a person is to be treated as a non-Christian if he or she refuses to listen to the church (v. 17)?

Jesus places a high priority on the church. We are to work and struggle to get along. But if offenders spurn the advice of the church, they are cutting themselves off not only from the church but from God as well.

7. How does the presence of Jesus among his people (vv. 18 – 19) relate to the process of reconciliation?

According to Jesus, reconciliation requires more than patience and forgiveness. Mercy has no meaning without authority and justice. This can be hard for us to understand in a relativistic society that is blind to moral absolutes. Our culture thinks justice and forgiveness are easy. As Christians we can think that way as well, forgetting the price Christ paid to forgive us and the requirement of repentance that he places on all who enter the kingdom of heaven.

8. Read verses 21 – 35. What is the connection between Jesus' teaching on reconciliation and Peter's question about the frequency of forgiveness (v. 21)?

9. What is the difference between forgiving seven times and forgiving seventy-seven times (v. 22)?

The Greek could be translated "seven times seventy," conveying Jesus' point that our forgiveness of one another is to be unlimited.

10. How does the parable of the king and his servant illustrate God's patience and mercy toward us (vv. 23 – 27)?

11. After being forgiven his massive debt, why do you think the servant refused to be patient and merciful with his fellow servant (vv. 28 – 30)?

12. God is the master who has forgiven our massive debt of sin. How does the experience of being forgiven affect you?

13. Because God has forgiven us, Jesus requires that we forgive others (v. 35). What does it mean to forgive them "from your heart"?

PRAY ABOUT IT

As you consider someone who has offended you or sinned against you, ask God to give you the courage and resolve to speak to that person. Pray that the discussion that occurs opens the way for reconciliation and forgiveness.

TAKING THE NEXT STEP

Make a list of people with whom you have an unresolved issue. Pray through the list, asking God to show you with which person you ought to begin. Then come up with a plan for how to approach the person and resolve the issue.

STUDY 23

Waiting for the Lord

PSALM 40:1–5

I hate to wait.

Waiting in lines, waiting for a long-expected letter, waiting for a phone call, waiting for important information — they all bother me. Yet such things are merely an inconvenience. In his book *Waiting*, Ben Patterson calls us to look more deeply at the issue of waiting:

> There is another, more acute kind of waiting — the waiting of a childless couple for a child; the waiting of a single person for marriage or whatever is next; the waiting of the chronically ill for health or death; the waiting of the emotionally scarred for peace; the waiting of men and women in dead-end careers for a breakthrough; the waiting of unhappy marriages for relief or redemption or escape; the waiting of students to get on with life; the waiting of the lonely to belong.
>
> For Christians in these kinds of waitings, the question is "How long, O Lord?"[1]

WARMING UP

1. When have you been in a situation in which you had to wait for the Lord?

---

1. Ben Patterson, *Waiting: Finding Hope When God Seems Silent* (Downers Grove, Ill.: InterVarsity Press, 1989), 9–10.

DIGGING IN

2.   Read Psalm 40:1 – 5. David waited patiently for the Lord's help (v. 1). What is the difference between waiting patiently and waiting impatiently?

One dictionary defines *impatience* as "not willing to put up with delay." Another definition is "annoyance."

Although David waits patiently (v. 1), he also asks the Lord not to delay (see v. 17). His request for speedy deliverance is not the same as impatience. There is nothing wrong with asking the Lord to come quickly to our rescue. Yet if he fails to do so, and we become angry and bitter, that is an expression of impatience.

3.   Why is waiting patiently for the Lord often difficult?

4.   David was in a slimy pit and a muddy mire — hardly a place to wait patiently! What do you think he was feeling in such circumstances?

5.   What "slimy pits" have caused you to cry out to the Lord?

6.   God delivered David from the slimy pit and set his feet on a rock (v. 2). What "rocks" has God provided in response to your prayers?

7.   Patient waiting requires trust (vv. 3 – 4). What does it mean to put your trust in the Lord?

We trust the Lord for our eternal life beyond sin and death. We must also trust him for daily bread and for help in the life crises that we face. A good way to tell how well we trust him to save us from eternal death is to evaluate how much we trust him to help us in the painful events of our daily lives.

8.   When we tell others about God's help (v. 3), their faith and ours is strengthened. How does David's account of God's deliverance strengthen your faith?

9.   What can you tell others about God's help in your life so that their faith can be strengthened?

10. Why is there such a strong temptation to look to others for help rather than to God (v. 4)?

What "gods" are you tempted to look to when you are in trouble?

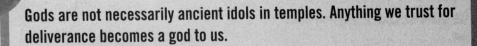

Gods are not necessarily ancient idols in temples. Anything we trust for deliverance becomes a god to us.

11. It is important to see God's involvement in the everyday events of life. How does your ability to see God's "wonders" compare to David's (v. 5)?

PRAY ABOUT IT

Ask God to give you spiritual eyes to discern his shaping hand behind the frustrations and challenges that you face.

TAKING THE NEXT STEP

In verse 3 David celebrates God's deliverance with a new song. You may not be a poet or songwriter, but you can still worship the Lord with your own new song. Set aside some time to write out a few lines of praise to God. Perhaps you could begin by rewriting the first five verses of Psalm 40 in your own words. Then go on from there to describe how God has met your needs, and in so doing, celebrate his goodness.

Waiting until the End

ROMANS 8:18–30

"In two months we hope to ..." "In a year we hope that ..." Hope for the future. Without it, we give up. With it, we keep going.

Hope for a vacation can keep us going when pressures at work become a heavy burden. If we can't see any break in the job, we may conclude it is better just to quit. Hope for a cure can provide strength to face an otherwise intolerable level of pain. Pain that seems endless crushes any desire to go on living.

We all need hope. But hope for next year or even ten years ahead is not enough. We need a far greater hope for the future. The apostle Paul writes of such a hope in the concluding portion of Romans 8.

WARMING UP

1.   What are some of the things that you hope for?

DIGGING IN

2. Read Romans 8:18 – 30. Paul writes that present sufferings are nothing compared to our hope of future glory. Consider the phrases *subjected to frustration* and *bondage to decay* (vv. 20 – 21). What type of world do they describe?

3. Why do you think Paul places such emphasis on the physical world being restored (vv. 18 – 21) before talking about the future benefits of our salvation (vv. 22 – 25)?

The Christian faith regards the physical as important. God is the maker of heaven and earth, the visible and the invisible. Further, this world is where we have been placed by God.

4. How would thinking about your troubles as birth pangs (v. 22) affect the way you view them?

5. What do the "family" words Paul uses, like *children of God* (vv. 19, 21), *childbirth* (v. 22), and *adoption to sonship* (v. 23), convey about our present and future as Christians?

6.　How has the Christian family been a help to you in facing hard times?

7.　Although we are already God's children (v. 16), what experiences still await us (v. 23)?

Adoption was common among the Greeks and Romans, who granted the adopted son all the privileges of a natural son, including inheritance rights.... Christians are already God's children, but this is a reference to the full realization of our inheritance in Christ. The resurrection is the final stage in our adoption.

The NIV Study Bible, notes on Romans 8:15, 23

Notice Paul's reference to "the firstfruits of the Spirit" (v. 23). Like the firstfruits of a harvest, the Holy Spirit is a pledge of more and greater things to come. Likewise, he is a down payment of our future inheritance.

8.　What causes you to "groan" (v. 23) as you wait for God to complete his work in your life?

9.　Hope is central to the Christian faith (vv. 24–25). From these verses, how would you define Christian hope?

10. How is it possible to wait both eagerly (v. 23) and patiently (v. 25) for our hopes to be fulfilled?

11. As we wait, how does the Holy Spirit help us with our weakness and groaning (vv. 26–27)?

> While having the Spirit removes us from the power of sin, it also puts us into a struggle with sin, a struggle that can lead to inward groaning.

12. How does it help you to know that the Spirit is praying for you during your struggles?

13. The ultimate future for which we wait is something we can count on because it is grounded in the plan of God (vv. 28–30). How does knowing that all things work together for good give you a sense of hope?

If God is at work in all things, does that mean he is the cause of our troubles? The answer is no. Scripture is clear that God is not the cause of sin. However, because he is at work all the time, everywhere, nothing is beyond his power or his purpose. How these two truths fit together is not quite clear, but we don't have to understand it to benefit from the strength and comfort of our knowledge of this mystery.

PRAY ABOUT IT

Thank God for the hope we have in Christ. Ask him for the grace to wait for Christ's return with both eagerness and patience.

TAKING THE NEXT STEP

Make a list of the things that you hope for in the next ten years of your life. Next make a list of what you hope to do before your life is over. As you ponder your hopes for this life, consider how they reflect your background and character. Next consider how your hopes reflect your Christian faith. Finally, consider how your hopes will find fulfillment in the world to come.

Kindness

REACHING OUT
TO OTHERS

Phyllis J. LePeau

Introduction

Several years ago some seminary students were asked to preach on the story of the good Samaritan. When the hour arrived for their sermon, each one was deliberately delayed en route to class. As the students raced across campus, they encountered a person who pretended to be in need. Ironically, not one of the students stopped to help. After all, they had an important sermon to preach!

It's easy to laugh at the hypocrisy of those students. Yet every day in various ways we reenact Christ's parable. Whether it's a family on the side of the road with car trouble, a homeless person sleeping over an outdoor heating vent, or a panhandler asking for spare change — we either pass by or reach out in kindness.

These daily opportunities make me excited about exploring what the Bible says about kindness and goodness. (The two words/concepts are very close in both Hebrew and Greek, so we will consider them together in this study.)

What we discover is that the word for "kindness" is much richer in meaning than its English translation would suggest. The NIV translates the Hebrew word *hesed* as "kindness" (41 times), "love" (129 times), "unfailing love" (32 times), "unfailing kindness" (3 times), and "loving-kindness" (1 time). The Hebrew lexicon suggests that it can also be translated as "goodness." The Greek word is also rich and diverse in meaning. The word is broad because the kindness and love of God are broad, reaching out to those in need.

The Bible tells us that God's kindness is freely given, that it preserves us, and that it is "better than life." It involves the warmth of God's fellowship as well as the security of his goodness and faithfulness.

It certainly follows that if we experience God's kindness, we will be transformed by it and reach out in kindness to others. It is with this hope that we begin to explore this multifaceted fruit of the Spirit.

Of the six studies in this section, four look at *principles* of kindness and goodness: God's kindness to us, showing kindness to others, fulfilling the law of Christ, and reaching out to the poor and needy. And, because kindness is seen most clearly in real life, we will also look at two *examples* of kindness: the relationships between Ruth and Boaz and David and Mephibosheth.

As you reflect on each passage of Scripture, may you experience the Lord's kindness, be transformed by it, and demonstrate it to others.

God's Kindness to Us

PSALM 103

There are a lot of parallels between being children in a physical sense and being a child of God. One of the most blatant similarities is gratefulness — or the lack thereof. Children are often self-centered and at times are hardly aware of the kindness that is extended to them by their parents.

As God's children, our awareness and appreciation of his kindness should be as natural as breathing fresh air. Yet that is not always the case. We need eyes that see and hearts that believe that God's kindness extends to us. As you look closely at God's kindness in Psalm 103, ask him to open your eyes to all that is there.

WARMING UP

1.   What do you think it would be like never to have experienced God's kindness?

DIGGING IN

2.   Read Psalm 103. According to verses 2 – 5, what kind and loving things has God done for us?

All God does stems from who he is (*name*) and what he is (*holy*): He never acts outside what he has revealed and what he is.

Derek Kidner, *Psalms 73–150*, Tyndale Old Testament Commentaries

3. In this first paragraph (vv. 2–5), how does God's loving-kindness meet our physical, emotional, and spiritual needs?

The blend of changeless fatherly care and endless sovereign rule is the distinctive stress of this psalm.

The New Bible Commentary: Revised

4. Which of the Lord's "benefits" have you experienced recently? Explain.

Praise [v. 2] is the distinctive word "Bless." When the Lord blesses us, he reviews our *needs* and responds to them; when we bless the Lord, we review his *excellencies* and respond to them. (italics added)

The New Bible Commentary: Revised

5. As you read the psalmist's description of God in verses 6–14, what kind of portrait emerges?

6. How are God's kindness and love demonstrated in his treatment of the oppressed (vv. 6–7)?

7. How is God's loving-kindness revealed in the way he treats those who sin (vv. 8–12)?

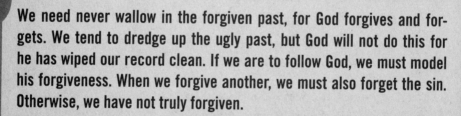

We need never wallow in the forgiven past, for God forgives and forgets. We tend to dredge up the ugly past, but God will not do this for he has wiped our record clean. If we are to follow God, we must model his forgiveness. When we forgive another, we must also forget the sin. Otherwise, we have not truly forgiven.

Life Application Bible, note on Psalm 103:12

"Forgetting" the sins of others that we have forgiven does not mean a sudden loss of memory. Rather, we determine never to hold that offense against the person who is forgiven. We do not dwell on the offense. The literal forgiving will follow.

8.   In what ways do you struggle with accepting God's forgiveness?

How can these verses help you to live in the freedom of his forgiveness?

9.   How does God respond to our frailty and mortality (vv. 13 – 19)?

10. How do his compassion and love reach even beyond the grave for those who fear him?

11. Reflect again on the ways God's loving-kindness has been shown to you according to this psalm. In what specific ways could you imitate his kindness in your relationships with others?

PRAY ABOUT IT

Praise to God is an appropriate way to open and close this psalm. Using verses 1 – 2 and 20 – 22 as your model, pray to God, praising him for his kindness, love, and compassion. Ask him to produce in you the fruit of kindness.

TAKING THE NEXT STEP

Often in our prayer life, praise is short-lived as we move quickly to requests for both ourselves and others. Using Psalm 104 as a model, take several days to pray a prayer of praise to God. (You might want to write this prayer out below.) First praise him for every detail that you see in this psalm about who God is. Then praise him for his kind works. Finally, praise him for how you have been touched by who he is and what he has done.

Showing Kindness to Others

MATTHEW 10:40–42; MARK 9:33–37

According to Greek mythology, the god Jupiter decided to find out how hospitable the people of Phrygia were. He and his companion, Mercury, dressed as poor wayfarers and wandered from door to door, asking for food and a place to rest. At every house they were treated rudely, and doors were slammed in their faces.

At last they came to the poorest hovel and were greeted by a kindly-faced old man named Philemon and his wife, Baucis. The couple welcomed them warmly and invited them in. They gave them seats by the fire and hurried to make them a meal. Although the couple had only diluted wine to offer, they eagerly refilled their guests' cups as soon as they were empty.

Because of the couple's generous hospitality, Jupiter rewarded them richly. Their container of wine never ran dry, and their home was transformed into a temple, over which they were appointed as priests and guardians.

Although the story is myth, the principle it teaches is quite biblical: We should never underestimate the worth of our guests or the value of any act of kindness.

WARMING UP

1.   Are you ever tempted to treat some people better than others? Why?

DIGGING IN

2. Read Matthew 10:40 – 42. What various types of people does Christ view as his representatives?

What motivation are we given for "welcoming" each one?

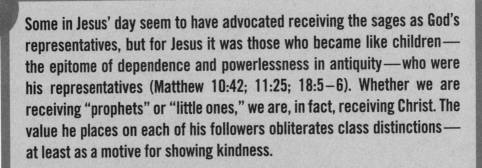

Some in Jesus' day seem to have advocated receiving the sages as God's representatives, but for Jesus it was those who became like children — the epitome of dependence and powerlessness in antiquity — who were his representatives (Matthew 10:42; 11:25; 18:5 – 6). Whether we are receiving "prophets" or "little ones," we are, in fact, receiving Christ. The value he places on each of his followers obliterates class distinctions — at least as a motive for showing kindness.

3. How would you respond if Christ himself came to your home, asking for food, shelter, or clothing?

4. How does it help you to know that by showing kindness to the least of Christ's followers, you are showing kindness to Jesus and his Father?

5.   Jesus mentions the word *reward* three times in three verses. What type of reward do you imagine you will receive for showing kindness to other Christians?

     Does the promise of a reward give you any additional motivation? Why or why not?

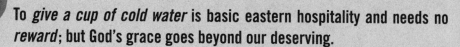

To *give a cup of cold water* is basic eastern hospitality and needs no *reward*; but God's grace goes beyond our deserving.

The New Bible Commentary: Revised

6.   Read Mark 9:33 – 37. Why do you suppose the disciples were arguing about who was the greatest?

7.   What are some of the marks and symbols of greatness in our culture?

8.   How does Jesus stand the world's concept of greatness on its head (v. 35)?

According to Jesus, the question is not whether we have many servants, but whether we serve many.

9. In what practical ways might you be "the very last, and the servant of all" at home and in your church?

10. Children had a lowly place in Jewish society (v. 36). What types of people are we inclined to view as lowly in our culture?

11. In what sense does Christ's statement (v. 37) obliterate such distinctions?

12. Think of one person you know who might be viewed as lowly by others. In what specific ways might you treat that person with kindness by receiving, welcoming, or giving a cup of cold water for Christ's sake?

PRAY ABOUT IT

Make a list of every Christian you know who might be perceived as lowly by those in our culture (e.g., missionaries). Pray for them daily for the next week.

TAKING THE NEXT STEP

In order to live a life of radical kindness in this world as representatives of Jesus, we must first relinquish the right to our own life. We "must be the very last, and the servant of all" (Mark 9:35). Write a paraphrase in your own words of the following passages that have to do with this radical lifestyle: Matthew 10:37 – 39; John 13:1 – 17; Philippians 2:1 – 11.

Ask God to build the fruit of kindness into you by integrating the truth of these passages into your life.

Kindness Illustrated: Boaz and Ruth
RUTH 2

The events in the book of Ruth are set in the time of the judges. That period spanned the first two or three centuries after Israel entered Canaan under Joshua's leadership. Because of a famine in Bethlehem, a man named Elimelek, his wife, Naomi, and their two sons migrated to the country of Moab. In the ten years that they lived there, the two sons married Moabite women, and then the two sons and their father died. Left alone and destitute, Naomi heard that the Lord had provided food in Judah. Naomi's daughter-in-law Ruth was willing to leave her family, homeland, and all that was comfortable to her because of her love and loyalty to Naomi. Together they traveled to Bethlehem.

Our study begins in chapter 2, where Ruth, though a foreigner in a strange land, is shown great kindness.

WARMING UP

1. Have you ever received kindness from a total stranger? How were you affected by that act of kindness?

DIGGING IN

2. Read Ruth 2. Ruth's commitment to Naomi was so great that she left all to go with her to a strange land. How does Ruth continue to demonstrate her loyalty?

> *Regarding verse 2:* Ruth, who knew nothing about Boaz, proposed to take advantage of the ancient law permitting the needy to glean in the fields at harvest time (cf. Leviticus 19:9, 23:22; Deuteronomy 24:19), so sparing Naomi the toil and humiliation such work involved.
>
> *The New Bible Commentary: Revised*

3. How do Ruth and Boaz meet?

4. Look closely at Boaz. What do you learn about him in verses 4 – 16?

5. Why does Boaz respond to Ruth in such a kind way (vv. 10 – 12)?

   How does Boaz describe the Lord to Ruth (v. 12)?

6.   What specific needs of Ruth does Boaz meet (vv. 14 – 18)?

In the case of Ruth, who had no brother-in-law, a more distant relative was supposed to marry her. When the Old Testament asserted that Yahweh was Israel's *Go'el* it underlined His covenant promise, by which Israel became His own possession (Exodus 19:5). He dwelt among His people (Exodus 25:8) and was their divine Kinsman, ready to deliver and protect them. The special contribution of this book is to make clear that the *go'el* alone possessed the right to redeem, and yet was under no obligation to do so. The willing, generous response of Boaz was, in a very small way, a foreshadowing of the great *Go'el*, who was to descend from him.

The New Bible Commentary: Revised

7.   How is Ruth affected by Boaz's kindness?

How would you have been affected by it?

8.   When have you been "put at ease" by someone's kindness?

9. In verses 19 – 22, what is Naomi's response to Boaz's kindness?

10. How is the rippling (multiplying) effect of kindness illustrated throughout this passage?

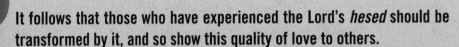

> It follows that those who have experienced the Lord's *hesed* should be transformed by it, and so show this quality of love to others.
>
> *The New Bible Commentary: Revised*

11. Think of someone in your family who needs to experience God's kindness through you. What are the first steps you need to take to show kindness to that person?

PRAY ABOUT IT

Ask God to allow the fruit of kindness to grow freely in you and to be demonstrated this week, especially in your family.

TAKING THE NEXT STEP

Often it is most difficult to express kindness to members of our family or to those with whom we closely live. Make a kindness plan for the people within your household. Plan one act of kindness a day. Record both their response and how you felt about it.

Fulfilling the Law of Christ

GALATIANS 6:1–10

In Truman Capote's *Other Voices, Other Rooms*, the hero is about to walk along a heavy but rotting beam over a brooding, murky creek. Starting over, "stepping gingerly … he felt he would never reach the other side: always he would be balanced here, suspended between land and in the dark and alone. Then feeling the board shake as Idabel started across, he remembered that he had someone to be together with. And he could go on."[1]

Having someone with us during hard times can make the difference between going on and giving up. In Galatians 6 Paul urges us to fulfill the law of Christ by carrying each other's burdens.

WARMING UP

1. Think of your closest friend. In what ways has he or she made life's burdens easier to bear?

---

1. As quoted by Maxie D. Dunnam, *Galatians, Ephesians, Philippians, Colossians, Philemon*, The Communicator's Commentary (Waco, Tex.: Word, 1982), 122.

DIGGING IN

2.   Read Galatians 6:1 – 10. What instructions does Paul give concerning some-one who is caught in a sin?

How would you feel if you were "caught in a sin" by members of your church?

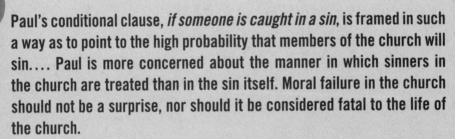

Paul's conditional clause, *if someone is caught in a sin*, is framed in such a way as to point to the high probability that members of the church will sin.... Paul is more concerned about the manner in which sinners in the church are treated than in the sin itself. Moral failure in the church should not be a surprise, nor should it be considered fatal to the life of the church.

G. Walter Hansen, *Galatians*, The IVP New Testament Commentary Series

3.   Why is gentleness extremely important in the response to someone caught in sin?

> Gentleness is not only consideration of the needs of others but also humility in recognition of one's own needs before God. So Paul moves from his command for restoration in the plural form, addressed to all, to a command for self-examination in the singular form, addressed to each individual. Corporate responsibility must be undergirded by the personal integrity of each individual before God.
>
> Hansen, *Galatians*

4. Paul urges us to "carry each other's burdens" (v. 2). What types of burdens often press down on or even crush you and/or people around you?

5. In what specific ways might you make their burden lighter? How could someone else help make your burdens lighter?

6. In what sense do we "fulfill the law of Christ" (v. 2) by carrying each other's burdens?

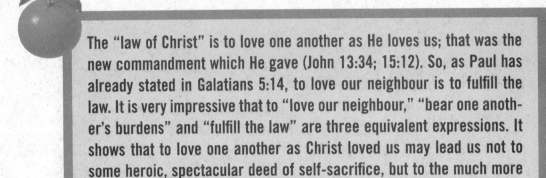

The "law of Christ" is to love one another as He loves us; that was the new commandment which He gave (John 13:34; 15:12). So, as Paul has already stated in Galatians 5:14, to love our neighbour is to fulfill the law. It is very impressive that to "love our neighbour," "bear one another's burdens" and "fulfill the law" are three equivalent expressions. It shows that to love one another as Christ loved us may lead us not to some heroic, spectacular deed of self-sacrifice, but to the much more mundane and unspectacular ministry of burden-bearing.

John R. W. Stott, *The Message of Galatians*, The Bible Speaks Today

7.   How might restoring those who sin or carrying others' burdens lead us to feel proud (v. 3)?

8.   What does Paul say we should do to avoid this pitfall (vv. 4 – 5)?

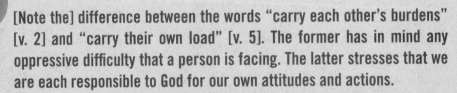

[Note the] difference between the words "carry each other's burdens" [v. 2] and "carry their own load" [v. 5]. The former has in mind any oppressive difficulty that a person is facing. The latter stresses that we are each responsible to God for our own attitudes and actions.

Jack Kuhatschek, *Galatians: Why God Accepts Us*

9.   What do you think is involved in testing your own actions?

10. What obligations do we have toward those who instruct us in the Word (v. 6)?

What kinds of "good things" do you think Paul has in mind?

11. At first, it seems that Paul's warnings about sowing and reaping come out of nowhere (vv. 7 – 9). How does his analogy relate to doing good to others?

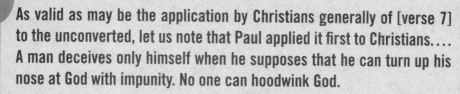

As valid as may be the application by Christians generally of [verse 7] to the unconverted, let us note that Paul applied it first to Christians.... A man deceives only himself when he supposes that he can turn up his nose at God with impunity. No one can hoodwink God.

The New Bible Commentary: Revised

12. Why might we become weary and be tempted to give up as we express kindness to those in need (vv. 7 – 9)?

13. Give one specific example of how you might live out the fruit of kindness in the life of a Christian or non-Christian you know.

PRAY ABOUT IT

Thank God for the community of believers in which he has placed you. Pray that the Holy Spirit will make you aware of specific ways that you can express the fruit of kindness to people within your community.

TAKING THE NEXT STEP

Write a letter of encouragement and affirmation to your pastor. Include such things as your appreciation for his/her study of the Scriptures, teaching, faithful service to the congregation, character, integrity, and love for the Lord.

STUDY 29

Reaching Out to the Poor and Needy
PROVERBS 14:21, 31; 19:17

Hudson Taylor, famous missionary to China and founder of the China Inland Mission, was called to a home to pray for a sick woman. He was called because, unlike other religious leaders of the day, he did not charge the family to pray for her.

The woman was very poor. When Taylor saw her poverty, he clutched the coin in his pocket. It was the only money he had. He wished that there were two so he could give one to her. After all, he could not give her his only coin! What would he do to survive? He had only two meals left at home for himself.

He knelt to pray for the woman but found that he could not pray. God was asking him to give up his precious coin. He tried again to pray. How could he walk away with nothing to live on? Again, he could not pray. Finally, he gave her the coin. He was released by God and felt great freedom and blessing as he prayed.

Hudson Taylor's experience provides one example of what it means to reach out to the poor and needy—something God asks from us even when we are poor and needy ourselves.

WARMING UP

1.   Who are some of the poor and needy that live in your area?

DIGGING IN

2. Read Proverbs 14:21. Do you tend to view the needy as your neighbors? Why or why not?

The proverbs use a device known as poetic parallelism, in which elements in the first line are restated and amplified in the second line. In Proverbs 14:21 our neighbors and the needy are the same group.

3. What acts of kindness might we show to those in need?

4. How have you felt God's blessing as a result of being kind to the needy?

5. Read Proverbs 14:31. In what ways are the poor oppressed in our society?

Why do you think so many have so little materially, while a few have so much?

6. When have you oppressed the poor, either directly or indirectly?

7. "Shows contempt for their Maker" are strong words. Why do you think oppressing the poor shows contempt for God?

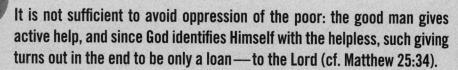

It is not sufficient to avoid oppression of the poor: the good man gives active help, and since God identifies Himself with the helpless, such giving turns out in the end to be only a loan—to the Lord (cf. Matthew 25:34).

The New Bible Commentary: Revised

8. Conversely, how does being kind to the needy honor God?

9. Read Proverbs 19:17. In what sense are we loaning to the Lord when we are kind to the poor?

10. Do you think our "reward" is something we will receive now, in the future, or both? Explain.

[Proverbs 19:17] promises faithful recompense, not necessarily one's money back!

Derek Kidner, *Proverbs*, Tyndale Old Testament Commentaries

11. What do these proverbs reveal about God's concern for the poor?

What actions and attitudes toward the poor do you think God expects from us?

12. What specific ways can you honor God this week by being kind to the poor and needy?

PRAY ABOUT IT

Confess your sin of oppressing the poor. Ask the Lord to reveal to you any ways that you oppress the poor that you may not be aware of. Thank him for his love for the poor and needy and for his forgiveness to you.

TAKING THE NEXT STEP

Investigate opportunities for serving the poor through a soup kitchen, food pantry, or homeless shelter. Volunteer to serve at one of these places for an afternoon.

Kindness Illustrated: David and Mephibosheth

2 SAMUEL 9

We have very special friends coming to live with us this summer. We are excited about the time we will have with them. We are also anticipating a great time with their three sons, though we have never met them. Because we love Jackie and Steve, we love Jeremy, Chris, and Justin and have already decided to embrace them as our own children. Because of our love for and loyalty to their parents, the boys have a place in our hearts.

So it was with David. Because of David's deep love for Jonathan, David went out of his way to show kindness to Jonathan's son Mephibosheth.

WARMING UP

1. When have you shown kindness to someone you did not know? Why?

DIGGING IN

2. What do you know about David and Jonathan's relationship? (Glance through 1 Samuel 18:1 – 4; 19:1 – 5; and 20:1 – 23 for more information.)

How would you describe their love for and loyalty to each other?

3.   Read 2 Samuel 9. What steps did David go through to find Mephibosheth (vv. 1 – 5)?

4.   What motivated David to find him and show kindness to him?

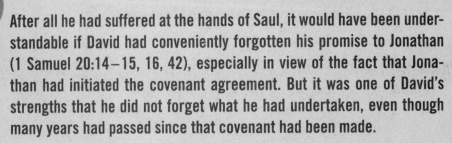

After all he had suffered at the hands of Saul, it would have been understandable if David had conveniently forgotten his promise to Jonathan (1 Samuel 20:14 – 15, 16, 42), especially in view of the fact that Jonathan had initiated the covenant agreement. But it was one of David's strengths that he did not forget what he had undertaken, even though many years had passed since that covenant had been made.

Joyce Baldwin, *1 and 2 Samuel*, Tyndale Old Testament Commentaries

5.   How does your love for and loyalty to a person motivate you to show kindness to his or her relatives?

6.   How would you describe Mephibosheth?

Why would he be an unlikely candidate to receive kindness from David?

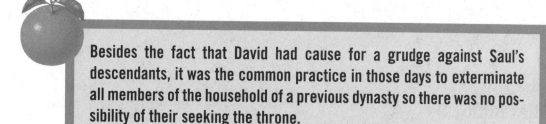

Besides the fact that David had cause for a grudge against Saul's descendants, it was the common practice in those days to exterminate all members of the household of a previous dynasty so there was no possibility of their seeking the throne.

7.   How extensive were the needs that David met?

8.   Verse 3 states that David wanted to show God's kindness. How is David's kindness to Mephibosheth like God's kindness to us?

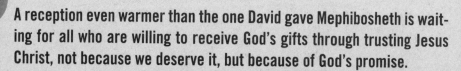

A reception even warmer than the one David gave Mephibosheth is waiting for all who are willing to receive God's gifts through trusting Jesus Christ, not because we deserve it, but because of God's promise.

Life Application Bible, note on 2 Samuel 9:5 – 6

9. Describe a situation in which you experienced God's kindness through a person you did not know. How were you affected?

10. David took risks in showing kindness to Mephibosheth. What risks do we take when we express kindness to people?

PRAY ABOUT IT

Think of someone who needs to experience God's kindness through you. Ask God to give you opportunities to express his kindness to that person.

TAKING THE NEXT STEP

Think about a friend who is a single parent or one who is caring for an elderly parent. Show God's kindness to that person by doing such things as helping with child care, visiting, calling, writing a note of encouragement, fixing a meal, or bringing in groceries.

Faithfulness

THE FOUNDATION OF
TRUE FRIENDSHIP

Jacalyn Eyre

Introduction

"Where do we go from here?" Our family had just moved to England on a limited ministry assignment. Because we would only be there a year or so, we had decided not to bring our furniture. So my husband and I and our three boys undertook our adventure with two suitcases apiece.

We were staying with colleagues while we looked for a place to live. We exhausted the ads in the newspaper. Everything seemed too small or too expensive. In a new country without familiar resources, we felt very disoriented and vulnerable.

From out of the blue, a woman stepped from the crowd at the church where we were visiting. She introduced herself as Sue and proceeded to ask enough questions to know everything about us. Then, much to our surprise, she warmly offered her services. She helped us find a house, negotiate terms, connect the utilities, and locate furniture, and she provided transportation. Two weeks after our initial meeting we were comfortably settled in the perfect house for our family.

We continued to benefit from Sue's hospitality through our entire stay in England. There were times when we felt we asked too much and when we feared we were imposing. But we never got any such signals from our "hostess." She and her family were there to continue to welcome and receive us. The message spoken and lived was, "You can depend on us."

God values such faithful friendships. In fact, God is the source and standard of friendship. In the Old Testament, God demonstrates the meaning of faithfulness as he calls Abraham, encourages Joshua, and forgives and loves Israel.

In the New Testament, Jesus is our model of faithfulness. He is not only the Lord of the disciples but also their friend. Jesus tells them in John 15:15, "I no longer call you servants, because a servant does not know his master's business. Instead, I have called you friends."

Scripture also contains numerous examples of men and women who committed themselves to God and to each other and who became faithful friends. Joshua worked for years as a faithful friend and aid to Moses. Ruth was a faithful companion to Naomi when life seemed filled with death, failure, and hopelessness. Jonathan was the friend of David and helped him even at the cost of Saul's anger and Jonathan's own claim to the throne. Barnabas was a faithful friend to the apostle Paul and was there to sponsor him when Paul was held in suspicion by the early church.

The faithful friendships between these people in the Scriptures brought blessings beyond measure. Joshua became the general who led Israel into the Promised Land. Ruth married into the nation of Israel and became the great-grandmother of King David and part of the line leading to the Messiah. Jonathan's friendship with David opened the way for David to become the great king whose ultimate heir would be Jesus Christ. And Barnabas launched Paul into a ministry that spread the gospel through the Roman Empire.

We all need faithful friends. And just as important, we need to learn to be faithful in our friendships. As you work through this section of *Fruit of the Spirit*, you will discover that faithfulness includes a commitment to be there the way Ruth was for Naomi; a willingness to forgive the way Hosea forgave his adulterous wife; a promise of support the way God supported Joshua as he led Israel; an honoring of commitments the way God required of Israel in a time of social decay; and a fulfilling of responsibilities the way Jesus taught his disciples just before his crucifixion. Finally, because faithfulness is difficult, we need to know that there are rewards for those who make the determined effort.[1]

May God cause the fruit of faithfulness to grow in all of your relationships.

---

1. Background material for this study comes from *The Message of Ruth: The Bible Speaks Today*, by David Atkinson; *The Expositor's Bible Commentary*, vols. 3, 5, 7, 8, by Frank E. Gaebelein; *Hosea*, Tyndale Old Testament Commentaries, by David Allan Hubbard; *Haggai, Zechariah, Malachi*, Tyndale Old Testament Commentaries, by Joyce G. Baldwin; *Matthew*, Tyndale New Testament Commentaries, by Richard France; *The Gospel of Matthew*, Tyndale New Testament Commentaries, by R. V. G. Tasker, and *The New Bible Commentary: Revised*.

A Commitment to Be There

RUTH 1

There is an old saying that when times are hardest you know who your friends are. That summarizes the first chapter of the book of Ruth.

Naomi's situation was at its worst. She had lost her husband and sons, which meant that she had also lost her source of income, security, and identity. She was without hope. It is at this point that Ruth, her daughter-in-law, does an astonishing thing—she decides to stay with Naomi. Ruth demonstrates a commitment to be there.

WARMING UP

1.   Why is faithfulness an important quality in friendship?

DIGGING IN

2.   Read Ruth 1. What do we learn about Naomi in verses 1–5?

In the Old Testament a Hebrew woman was her husband's possession. Although she was more than a slave, she had very few rights, and no inheritance rights. Any position of respect in the community grew out of the male children she bore. The word translated "widow" communicates loneliness, abandonment, and helplessness. The only hope of recovery of social status for a widow was to marry a second time.

3.   Ruth and Orpah are introduced as Naomi's daughters-in-law (v. 4). What basis do these three women have for mutual trust (vv. 1 – 5)?

The name Ruth is traditionally derived from *ra'ah*, a word meaning "friend" or "friendship."

4.   Consider a time when you shared a difficult experience with someone. How did it strengthen your friendship?

5.   What do verses 6 – 13 reveal about Naomi's relationship to God?

6.   When you have faced a painful experience, how has it affected your attitude toward God?

7.   The famine is over, and Naomi prepares to return to Bethlehem with her daughters-in-law. Why does Naomi encourage Ruth and Orpah to stay in Moab (vv. 8 – 14)?

While God had made provisions in the law for foreigners, they were not particularly welcome and were usually excluded from the life of the community. For example, marriage to a Moabite was not forbidden by law (Deuteronomy 7:1, 3), though a Moabite was not allowed in the congregation of the Lord to the tenth generation (Deuteronomy 23:3; Nehemiah 13:1 – 3).

8.   What cost does Naomi face by encouraging Ruth and Orpah to stay in Moab?

How do both Ruth and Orpah show faithfulness to Naomi by their different responses?

The word *clung* (v. 14) is a verb meaning a committed, faithful "cleaving" in a deep personal relationship.

9.   What does it cost you to be faithful to those you love?

10.   Read Ruth's familiar words in verses 16 – 17. How would you summarize her words of dedication?

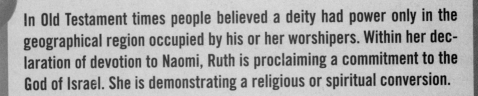

In Old Testament times people believed a deity had power only in the geographical region occupied by his or her worshipers. Within her declaration of devotion to Naomi, Ruth is proclaiming a commitment to the God of Israel. She is demonstrating a religious or spiritual conversion.

11.   Naomi's homecoming is painful (vv. 19 – 22). How does Naomi view herself and her situation?

12. What provisions has God made for Naomi even in the midst of this bitter time?

13. In what situations is it most important for us to be there for our loved ones and friends?

How does Ruth's example encourage you to be faithful in good times and in bad?

PRAY ABOUT IT

Our Father, teach us to recognize and understand friendship. Teach us how to receive friendship. Teach us how to be a friend. Like Naomi, give us the capacity to know, show, and speak our feelings—love, anger, longing, bitterness, despair, and devotion. Like Orpah, give us the ability to separate from those we love if it is required of us. Like Ruth, who reflects your character, give us the courage to be faithful; to give support, love, and commitment; and to cling to those you call into our lives. May we show kindness especially to those who feel judged and rejected. Father, teach us friendship. Teach us faithfulness.

TAKING THE NEXT STEP

According to *The American Heritage Dictionary of the English Language*, third edition, faithfulness is the act of "adhering firmly and devotedly, as to a person, a cause, or an idea." Synonyms are *loyal, true, constant, fast, steadfast, staunch.*

Faithfulness suggests undeviating attachment. Close your eyes, sit quietly, and imagine yourself in a conversation with God about faithfulness. If you have any questions, ask them. Afterward, record this conversation. Spend a few moments in reflection.

List times when you have been angry with God or felt deserted by him, even judged by him. Now list ways in which God has been faithful to you. List ways you have been faithful to God. When and how did you make your first commitment to God?

Ruth's commitment to Naomi seems extreme, yet this type of commitment is often made in marriage and many times in friendships. Make a list of those who are dear to you. In times when you felt empty, how have they been faithful to you? What kindnesses have they shown you? In times when you rejoiced, who has been with you to share your celebration? In what ways have you shown faithfulness and loyalty to your friends?

Spend time in thanksgiving. Thank God for your relationship with him and for the faithfulness he has shown you. Thank him for the people he has given you to love and for their friendship.

Shallow relationships characterize our culture. Job transfers from city to city expand our contacts but keep our roots shallow. It is easy just to think about finding new friends when we run into problems with our current ones.

God isn't like that. As we see from the book of Hosea, God makes commitments for both time and eternity. Through the faithful prophet Hosea, who reclaims his adulterous wife, God shows what lengths he is willing to go to in forgiving and being faithful to us.

WARMING UP

1. Why do you think forgiveness is one of the foundations of friendship?

DIGGING IN

2. Read Hosea 2:19 – 3:5. Looking back at 2:13, how would you describe the spiritual condition of Israel?

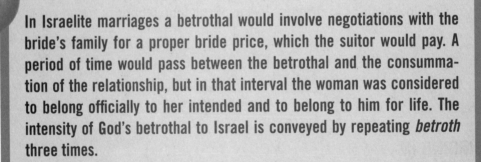

The events in Hosea took place during the reign of Jeroboam II, king of Israel. It was a prosperous time, and Hosea's prophecy of coming judgment must have seemed far-fetched. Israel adopted a Canaanite lifestyle, which included worship of their gods. The Baals of the Canaanites were regarded as a source of fertility and prosperity. Orgiastic worship at the shrines was the centerpiece of their religion. In essence, such religion was the opposite of everything embodied in God's covenant.

3. The word *betroth* is used three times in verses 19–20. What virtues and qualities characterize this commitment?

In Israelite marriages a betrothal would involve negotiations with the bride's family for a proper bride price, which the suitor would pay. A period of time would pass between the betrothal and the consummation of the relationship, but in that interval the woman was considered to belong officially to her intended and to belong to him for life. The intensity of God's betrothal to Israel is conveyed by repeating *betroth* three times.

4. God describes Israel's restoration in terms of marriage because he views idolatry as spiritual adultery. Why do you think God uses such a graphic term?

5. In what areas are God's people in our time and culture tempted to be unfaithful to God?

   In what areas do you struggle to be faithful to God?

6. The damaged relationship between God and Israel is repaired because God is willing to forgive. How would you describe the overflowing benefits that come from this reconciled relationship (vv. 21 – 23)?

7. Why can it be so difficult to forgive those who are close to us?

   What overflowing benefits result when we do forgive?

8. Hosea 3:1 – 5 focuses on Hosea and Gomer. Verse 1 tells how Gomer, though married to Hosea, is living with another man and worshiping other gods. God tells Hosea to reclaim his unfaithful wife. Given Hosea's situation, what do you think he would be thinking and feeling?

What reason does God give Hosea for this command to reclaim Gomer?

> The behavior of Gomer is not an indictment of the *women* of Israel, but of the *nation* of Israel. Hosea is commanded to love Gomer in spite of her unfaithfulness. Likewise, God will restore Israel in spite of her sin.

9.   Hosea must pay a price to reclaim Gomer (v. 2). How does Hosea's restoration of Gomer foreshadow the ministry of Jesus Christ?

10.   Forgiving love is costly. What price have you paid when forgiving another?

How does this passage motivate you to do whatever is necessary to forgive?

11.   How does this passage encourage you in your relationship to God?

PRAY ABOUT IT

"Our Father in heaven, hallowed be your name, your kingdom come, your will be done, on earth as it is in heaven. Give us today our daily bread. And forgive us our debts, as we also have forgiven our debtors. And lead us not into temptation, but deliver us from the evil one" (Matthew 6:9 – 13).

TAKING THE NEXT STEP

Consider times when, like Gomer, you were not in the least interested in God. What "Baals" drew your attention? What riches or rewards did you seek or experience from these gods? How did God draw you to himself, and how has he blessed you? How have you experienced God's forgiveness and faithfulness?

Make a list of the costs and benefits you have experienced in the process of forgiving a friend. Include in this list those to whom you need to extend forgiveness.

As you reflect on this list, move into a time of praise. Praise God for your ability to pay the cost and for the blessings that came out of that forgiveness. If you are unable to forgive, then petition God to give you the ability and grace to forgive. If this prayer is not answered quickly, be patient. You are precious in God's heart, and he is faithful.

A Promise of Support

JOSHUA 1:1 – 9

At our church we sing the words "Be bold, be strong, for the Lord your God is with you." My youngest son thought we were singing "Be bald, be strong ... "

As Joshua faced the daunting task of following Moses, I can imagine that he felt exposed and bald.

At times we all accept responsibilities that seem overwhelming. How well we perform frequently depends on the support and friendship of those around us.

In this chapter Joshua moves into a new "pastoral position" of leading over a million people. As the Lord promises to support Joshua, we observe a new facet of faithfulness and friendship.

WARMING UP

1. Recall a time when you took on a project or responsibility that seemed too massive. How did you feel?

DIGGING IN

2. Read Joshua 1:1–9. Moses is dead. How do you think Joshua would have felt about becoming Israel's leader after forty years of Moses' leadership?

Moses had an astounding relationship with God that shaped the nation forever. It would be difficult to overestimate his importance to Israel, but remember that Joshua was Moses' assistant. He saw Moses during his ordinary times. Joshua observed Moses' weaknesses, his stuttering, his temper, his disobedience, and his discouragements, as well as his great moments.

3. As Joshua begins to lead Israel into the Promised Land, what assurances does God give him (vv. 1–5)?

4. God promises to be with Joshua (v. 5). Why would that be encouraging?

5. What difference does it make when someone offers to come with you to accomplish a hard task?

6.   What does God require of Joshua in order to be successful and prosperous
     in leading Israel (vv. 6 – 9)?

The words "Do not turn from it [the law] to the right or to the left" (v. 7) communicate that there must be no deviation. The phrase "always on your lips" (v. 8) refers to the custom of muttering while reflecting or studying. When constantly muttering the law of God, Joshua would definitely be thinking about it.

7.   Joshua must meditate on the Law day and night (v. 8). How do you think
     this would help him to lead Israel?

8.   How have you been supported and strengthened by knowing the Scriptures?

9.   God tells Joshua not to be discouraged or afraid (v. 9). Why do you think this
     command was necessary?

10. How can God's command to be bold in the face of hard circumstances give us strength?

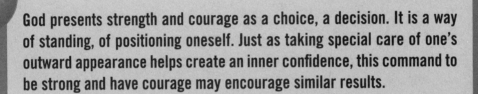

God presents strength and courage as a choice, a decision. It is a way of standing, of positioning oneself. Just as taking special care of one's outward appearance helps create an inner confidence, this command to be strong and have courage may encourage similar results.

11. Throughout this passage, how is the Lord himself a model of what it means to be a supportive friend?

12. Think of a friend who needs your support during a difficult time. How can you follow the Lord's example in helping that person?

PRAY ABOUT IT

Our Father, like Joshua, let us be open to your call on our lives. Your Son, Jesus, said to his eleven disciples, "All authority in heaven and on earth has been given to me. Therefore go and make disciples of all nations, baptizing them in the name of the Father and of the Son and of the Holy Spirit, and teaching them to obey everything I have commanded you. And surely I am with you always, to the very end of the age" (Matthew 28:18 – 20).

Like your disciples, let us hear and respond to your call on our lives no matter how large or how small. May each of us be strong and courageous, meditating on your Word day and night, remembering always your words, "I will never leave you nor forsake you" (Joshua 1:5).

TAKING THE NEXT STEP

"Be bold, be strong, for the Lord your God is with you." If you are going through a difficult time, sit quietly and close your eyes. Take a deep breath, then exhale. Picture God lifting you up and carrying you through this difficulty. With each breath, relax your body. God is with you. He will support your weight. He is faithful. (If your life is comfortable now, do this exercise considering a past struggle.)

Consider your friends. Make a list of how each has been supportive of you.

Think of a friend who needs your support. Ask God how you can show support to that friend. List possibilities.

Spend time praising God for his love, faithfulness, and support. Praise God for his promises and requirements and the benefits you experience from both. Thank God for your friends and what they mean to you.

Honoring Our Commitments

MALACHI 2:10–16

I promised a friend that I would care for her three children tonight while she attends a class. I would much prefer to spend the evening with a good book. I have had a very busy day, I am just getting over the flu, and dinner is waiting to be fixed.

Commitments are not always convenient. But God expects us to keep them. When we do, we benefit, others benefit, and God is pleased. In this study we look at a time in Israel when past commitments were not taken seriously and so were disregarded. In turn, Israel feared that God had abandoned his commitment to them. God speaks into this time of cynicism and unbelief to call Israel back to the covenant.

WARMING UP

1. Think of a time when someone broke a commitment to you. How did it make you feel?

DIGGING IN

2. Read Malachi 2:10 – 16. These verses are full of broken commitments. What specific commitments have been broken?

> Malachi was written in a "silent" time. The Jews returned from their Babylonian exile with high hopes. They rebuilt the temple and the walls of Jerusalem. As the years passed, however, they became disillusioned as the expected prosperity of their country did not come. They were surrounded by enemies, and they suffered drought, bad crops, and famine. They began to doubt God's love. They saw their enemies as being blessed and began to think that there was no profit in obedience. They became cynical, unbelieving, and gave up obedience to the law.

3. Consider the three questions posed in verse 10. What point is Malachi trying to make?

> The word *Father* is ambiguous. The NIV, by capitalizing the word, seems to imply that it refers to God. It is more probable that it refers to one of the patriarchs, as there is no precedent in the Old Testament for referring to God as Father in the manner that Jesus taught Christians to do. The word *father* probably refers to Jacob, since Malachi refers to Jacob in 1:2; 2:12; and 3:6.

4. Many churches struggle with internal conflicts. How could Malachi's questions help?

5. What is God's attitude toward Israel marrying "women who worship a foreign god" (v. 11)?

6. Intermarriage with pagans was strictly forbidden because it could lead to apostasy (see Exodus 34:15 – 16; Deuteronomy 7:3 – 4). How does this explain Malachi's seemingly harsh prayer in verse 12?

The Lord's objection to intermarriage is religious, not racial.

7. We are influenced by the people with whom we are closest (spouses, friends, business partners, and so on). What can we learn from verses 11 – 12?

8. The people are confused as to why God does not accept them (vv. 13 – 14). What is the problem (vv. 14 – 16)?

9. By observing key words or phrases like *unfaithful*, *partner*, and *marriage covenant* (vv. 14 – 15), what can we learn about God's view of marriage?

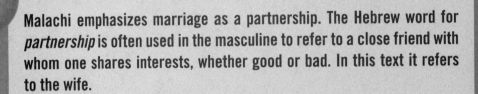

Malachi emphasizes marriage as a partnership. The Hebrew word for *partnership* is often used in the masculine to refer to a close friend with whom one shares interests, whether good or bad. In this text it refers to the wife.

10. How does God's view of marriage help us understand his attitude toward divorce (v. 16)?

11. How can knowing God's view of marriage enrich our own marriages (or our friendships)?

12. Healthy relationships require that we not be unfaithful to those to whom we have committed ourselves (vv. 15 – 16). How can honoring our commitments make a difference in the way we relate to our spouse or our friends?

PRAY ABOUT IT

Forgive us now, Father, as we humble ourselves before you, knowing we are unable to live up to the standards you place before us. Have mercy on us. We're grateful for the work of your Son, Jesus Christ, and that through him we are acceptable in your eyes. Flood our hearts with your love and hope. Give us the desire and ability to walk the path you place before us, keeping the faith with you, Father, and with our families and friends.

TAKING THE NEXT STEP

Consider what God has required of you. What commitments have you made to God? In what ways have you failed God? Yourself?

Healthy relationships require that we do not break faith with those to whom we have committed ourselves. Think of commitments you have made to family or friends. Which ones have you been careless about keeping? What can you do to better honor those commitments?

In quiet, spend time in confession asking God for forgiveness where you have fallen short of your commitments and obligations. Then picture a gentle waterfall flowing into a quiet pool surrounded by green hills. The water is the cleansing, refreshing work of the Holy Spirit. In your mind's eye, stand under the falls, swim in the pool, float, dive, do whatever you wish. This is God's healing space.

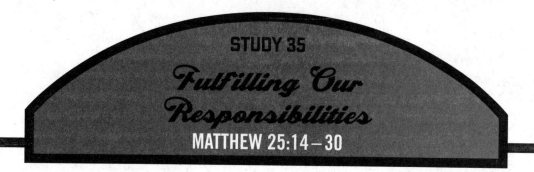

Fulfilling Our Responsibilities

MATTHEW 25:14–30

Friendship with others begins with our friendship with God. "You are my friends if you do what I command" (John 15:14). In all relationships there are commitments and obligations. This is especially true in our relationship with God.

In the parable of the talents, Jesus describes his expectations and requirements of his disciples. He calls us to make investments for him, to choose his goals, and then ultimately to "come and share" his happiness. We are called into a relationship of responsibility and friendship.

WARMING UP

1. What types of responsibility do you enjoy? What types of responsibility do you avoid?

DIGGING IN

2. Read Matthew 25:14–30. As the master leaves on a long journey, what resources does he give each of his servants (vv. 14–15) and what does he expect of them?

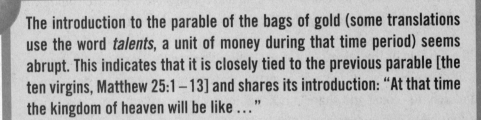

The introduction to the parable of the bags of gold (some translations use the word *talents*, a unit of money during that time period) seems abrupt. This indicates that it is closely tied to the previous parable [the ten virgins, Matthew 25:1–13] and shares its introduction: "At that time the kingdom of heaven will be like ..."

3. What are some of the resources Jesus has given to you?

What do you think Jesus expects of you?

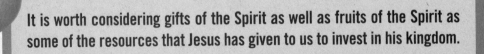

It is worth considering gifts of the Spirit as well as fruits of the Spirit as some of the resources that Jesus has given to us to invest in his kingdom.

4. How does the master show approval to the servants who please him (vv. 21, 23)?

In verse 19 the phrase "after a long time" is referring to the long delay of the consummation of the kingdom. As in the parable of the ten virgins, the servants must be watchful, resourceful, and persevering. The two servants who have been responsible with their master's wealth both receive verbal affirmation, increased responsibilities, and a share of their master's joy; however, they do not receive increased responsibility in equal amounts. The point of this parable is not egalitarianism, but the increase of responsibility and a share of the master's joy according to the ability of each. There is an emphasis in this parable of "from everyone who has been given much, much will be demanded" (Luke 12:48).

5. Recall a time when you sensed God's approval. What was it like?

6. How would you describe the behavior of the wicked servant (vv. 24 – 30)?

Why do you think the third servant did not invest his master's money?

The servant's irresponsible action betrays his lack of love for his master. In the end, the wicked servant blames the master himself for his own failure and excuses. The master exposes this servant as wicked and lazy. The message here is that even those who are given less are obligated to use and develop what they have. The third servant represents a discipleship of achieving nothing. Being faithful involves active, responsible service.

7.   What image does the third servant have of his master (vv. 24 – 25)?

How does our image of Jesus affect the way we serve him?

8.   How does the master show his disapproval (vv. 26 – 30)?

9.   The third servant receives a harsh judgment (vv. 28 – 30). What does Jesus want us to understand about our responsibilities within his kingdom?

10. What investments can you make for the sake of God's kingdom?

11. From this passage, what can we learn about our relationship with Jesus?

How can these principles be applied to our other friendships?

PRAY ABOUT IT

Quietly reflect on this passage, on the Father, Jesus, your responsibilities, and God's joy. Close your reflection time by reading John 15:9 – 15 and offering the following prayer: Our Father who is in heaven, holy is your name. Your kingdom come; your will be done on earth as it is in heaven. You, Father, are all-powerful, and your Son, Jesus, shares in all your glory. We are grateful for the friendship you offer us through Jesus and the responsibilities you give to us. We pray that we may honor you as we invest in your kingdom. Give us wisdom and perseverance as we love and serve you.

TAKING THE NEXT STEP

How is God requiring you to be responsible with the opportunities he has given you? What would God like you to invest in his kingdom? Speak to God about your desire to be faithful. Over the next few days, listen. What thoughts and ideas come to mind? Write them down. Then consider how to get started.

Relating this passage to our friendships is difficult because the parable speaks of a master/servant relationship. In our relationships, we do not and should not have the same level of responsibilities and consequences as we do with God; however, friendships do involve responsibilities and obligations. List the responsibilities you believe God has given you regarding a specific friend.

As you consider your investments in God's kingdom and your responsibilities toward a friend, remember you will find the ability to accomplish God's tasks in your relationship to God (see John 15:5 – 8).

The Rewards of Faithfulness

PROVERBS 3:3 – 4; 16:6; 20:28; 25:19

Very early we discovered that our son Jeremy was motivated by rewards. A five-hour task could be reduced to five minutes if an appropriate reward was offered.

Faithfulness is a lifelong task that requires continual effort. In the selected proverbs of this study, God shows us that there are rich rewards for those who do the hard work.

WARMING UP

1.   What benefits are there in being faithful to a friend?

DIGGING IN

2.   Read Proverbs 3:3 – 4; 16:6; 20:28; and 25:19. What are some of the benefits of faithfulness?

The word *faithful* can also be translated as "true." The central idea is that one who is faithful and conforms to the standard of God's law is therefore straight and true, not crooked, bent, or falling short.

3.   Faithfulness is paired with love in three of the four references. How are the two words complementary?

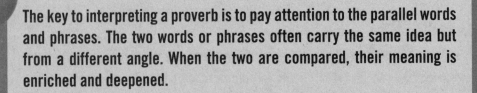

The key to interpreting a proverb is to pay attention to the parallel words and phrases. The two words or phrases often carry the same idea but from a different angle. When the two are compared, their meaning is enriched and deepened.

4.   According to Proverbs 3:3 – 4, what efforts does it take to gain and keep a good reputation?

5.   What are some of the benefits of a good reputation?

What are the liabilities of a poor reputation?

6.   Proverbs 16:6 says that faithfulness can help us overcome past sins against God and others. How do you think this works in practice?

This verse uses synonymous parallelism. The first half speaks of atonement for sin and the second half avoidance of sin. The emphasis is on complete freedom from sin.

7.   Fear of the Lord is parallel with faithfulness in this proverb. How are faithfulness and fear of the Lord complementary truths?

8.   How can faithfulness help us to live a godly life?

9.   Look at Proverbs 20:28. Love and faithfulness aren't traditionally hot topics on the political circuit. How would they contribute to a healthy government?

The idea here is that faithful covenant love brings stability to society.

10. How would it affect your attitude toward government to know that your political leaders were seeking to act in love and faithfulness?

11. Reread Proverbs 25:19. How do a bad tooth and a lame foot describe what it is like to depend on an unfaithful person?

12. We have all had the experience of being let down by someone. How are you affected? How do you tend to respond?

13. A life full of faithfulness is a rich life. How do the practical benefits of faithfulness motivate you to be a more faithful person to God and to your friends?

PRAY ABOUT IT

Father, create in me a heart that desires you. Teach me faithfulness that I may "win favor and a good name" in your sight and before humankind. Teach me to fear you that I may avoid evil and sin. Forgive me for my unfaithful times so that I may begin again fresh and cleansed. May I faithfully walk in your love all the days of my life.

TAKING THE NEXT STEP

David's twenty-third psalm expresses God's faithfulness to David. In it, David is confident that God is involved in every aspect of his life, both good and bad. David sees God as a shepherd, a guide, a protector, a friend. Using your own images and life experiences to express how God has been faithful to you, write your own psalm. Include the names of friends God has brought into your life. Honor God for his faithfulness.

Consider the previous studies in this section and the commitments you have made to God and friends. If you have begun to fulfill these commitments, be encouraged and continue on your adventure of faithfulness with God. If not, now is your beginning. Choose one commitment and start today.

Gentleness

THE STRENGTH OF BEING TENDER

Phyllis J. LePeau

Introduction

When Sis Levin's husband, Jerry, was kidnapped by Lebanese terrorists, she remained in Lebanon to seek his release. Instead of hostility, demands, and accusations against the people who held Jerry's life in their hands, she responded in gentleness. She cared for the children of that country and brought music to a cultural center established for them. She loved the people. At the time she was not aware of the strength of her tenderness.

While she was caring for these children, Jerry's normal crusts of bread and small pieces of cheese were suddenly replaced with warm food, fruit, and chocolate. His captors brought him extra socks and blankets. They even asked him what he wanted for a Christmas present. He requested and received a Bible.

Finally, he was allowed to escape. It wasn't until Sis and Jerry were together that Jerry knew why these sudden changes had taken place.

Gentleness is a vital necessity in many of our relationships in life — relationships with people in whom change comes very slowly, if at all. Often, instead of being gentle with them, we are harsh, abrupt, or defensive.

Yet we cannot grit our teeth and make ourselves into gentle people. It is truly a fruit. Gentleness can be produced in us only by the Spirit of God. Therefore, we simply and humbly admit our need and search the Scriptures for God's perspective on gentleness.

This section of *Fruit of the Spirit* is for people who, like me, want the fruit of gentleness to grow in them. We will begin by considering the fact that gentleness is not weakness. Next we will explore what it is to be gentle with the weak, with our words, and in our ministry. Finally, we will look at the gentleness of wisdom and the relationship between gentleness and power. I hope you will enjoy discovering more about gentleness, and may we learn together how to experience this vital fruit of the Spirit.

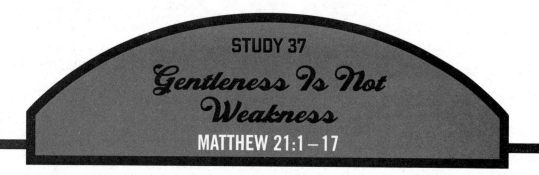

Gentleness Is Not Weakness

MATTHEW 21:1–17

"Gentle Jesus, meek and mild, look upon a little child." Jesus is often portrayed as gentle in poems, hymns, and paintings. Yet his "gentleness" seems limp, almost effeminate. His pale white skin and his delicate features make him seem soft, weak, retiring.

What a contrast to the Jesus of Scripture! In Matthew 21 we discover that there is strength in his gentleness and gentleness in his strength.

WARMING UP

1. Why do you think people sometimes assume that a gentle person is also a weak person?

DIGGING IN

2. Read Matthew 21:1–17. What impact do you think the events in verses 1–11 had on the disciples? On the crowd?

3. According to verse 5, the prophet Zechariah describes Jesus as gentle (Zechariah 9:9). How is his gentleness demonstrated in the way he approaches Jerusalem (vv. 5 – 11)?

The idea [of Christ's gentleness] is further elaborated by the description of His advent upon an untamed colt. The allusion to Genesis 49:10, 11 is clear. Judah will produce a mysterious ruler, who is not a worldly conqueror but will maintain his right by peaceful means. The contrast is strongly marked between the [donkey] and the war-horse, the emblems of peace and war respectively.

The New Bible Commentary: Revised

4. There is a sudden change of tone as Jesus enters the temple. What motivates Jesus' actions in verses 12 – 13?

Merchants and moneychangers set up their booths in the Court of the Gentiles in the Temple, filling it with their wares instead of allowing it to be filled with Gentiles who had come to worship God. The merchants sold sacrificial animals at high prices, taking advantage of those who had come long distances. The moneychangers exchanged all secular currency for Temple currency — the only kind of money the merchants would accept. They often deceived foreigners who didn't know the exchange rate.

The Life Application Bible, note on Matthew 21:12

5. How do Christ's actions in the temple contrast with the popular image of "gentle Jesus, meek and mild"?

6. In what kinds of situations is a firm, tough love more appropriate than a gentle response?

7. How is Christ's gentleness again demonstrated in his response to the blind, the lame, and the children (vv. 14–15)?

8. The chief priests and the teachers of the law are "indignant" when they see the wonderful things Jesus does and when they hear the shouts of the children (vv. 15–16). Why are the religious leaders threatened by these things?

The words of the children, which echo those of the crowds (v. 9), come primarily from Psalm 118:25–26. *Son of David* is a messianic title that infuriated the religious leaders, especially since Jesus did works that were fitting for the Messiah. [They] feared that Jesus would win the support of the people and overthrow their religious system.

The New Bible Commentary: Revised

9. How would you evaluate Christ's response to their challenge (vv. 16 – 17)? Is he confrontational? Gentle? Both?

10. What do you learn about gentleness as you observe Jesus throughout this passage?

11. In what ways do you struggle to achieve a gentleness that is not weak and a strength that is not harsh?

PRAY ABOUT IT

Ask God to develop the fruit of gentleness within you as you seek to follow the example of Jesus.

TAKING THE NEXT STEP

Based on what you have seen in Matthew 21, write a clear description and definition of gentleness. List the characteristics of Jesus that you see in this passage as preparation for creating this definition. Then reflect upon and jot down situations and relationships in which you would like to see the fruit of gentleness grow in you. For the next week make notes on the ways you are growing in gentleness.

STUDY 38

Being Gentle with the Weak

MATTHEW 12:15–21

My friend Pattie is the principal of the school where our children attend. I love to see her discipline children. It both challenges and convicts me. Because most children, by nature, are transparent and vulnerable, they feel weak when they have done something wrong. Even so, when disciplining them, my tendency is to be quick, harsh, angry, impatient, frustrated. Pattie is always gentle. She deals with the offense head-on. The children know beyond a doubt the nature of the offense, its consequences, and what will happen in the future if they do it again. But they also know that they are forgiven and loved. Though they have been weak, they leave strengthened by her tenderness.

WARMING UP

1.　What common types of weakness do people experience?

DIGGING IN

2.   Read Matthew 12:15 – 21. As you read this passage, what are your initial impressions about Jesus?

> This section simultaneously contrasts the hatred of the Pharisees (v. 14) with Jesus' tranquility (v. 19) and gentleness (v. 20).
>
> D. A. Carson, *Matthew*, The Expositor's Bible Commentary

3.   What do you think it means that "he will not quarrel or cry out; no one will hear his voice in the streets" (v. 19)?

> Jesus did not seek controversy, though He sometimes had to engage it. ... He did not wish to publish His Messiahship in the wrong way.
>
> *The New Bible Commentary: Revised*

4.   What is it like for you to be around someone who seeks controversy or who proclaims truth in an assertive and abrasive manner?

5.   What do a "bruised reed" and a "smoldering wick" represent (v. 20)?

The double metaphor breathes compassion: the servant does not advance his ministry with such callousness to the weak that he breaks the bruised reed or snuffs out the smoldering wick (smoldering either because it is poorly trimmed or low on oil). This may include reference to Jesus' attitude to the sick (v. 15). But the last clause of verse 20 ("till he has brought justice through to victory") ... suggests something more — namely that he brings eschatological salvation to the "harassed and helpless" (9:36), the "weary and burdened" (11:28).

Carson, *Matthew*

6.   How does Jesus respond to each?

7.   When have you felt like a reed that was bruised or a wick that was about to go out?

What were helpful and unhelpful ways that people responded to you?

8.   How do you generally respond to those who are physically, emotionally, or spiritually weak?

How would you like to respond?

9.   Proclaiming and promoting justice is an important part of Jesus' ministry (vv. 18, 20). How does gentleness, especially to the weak, contribute to that mission?

PRAY ABOUT IT

Think about a relationship in which you are struggling to be gentle. Ask God's Spirit to develop the fruit of gentleness in you as you grow in that relationship.

TAKING THE NEXT STEP

Create a modern paraphrase of verses 18–21. Instead of featuring Jesus as being the main character, write it about yourself. Think through specifically how you, as a follower of Jesus, would look if these verses described you. For instance, what would it mean in your life for you to be a servant? To have God's Spirit reigning in you? To proclaim justice to the nations (v. 18)? What would it be like for you not to quarrel or cry out (v. 19)? To respond as he did to the bruised reeds and smoldering wicks in your life?

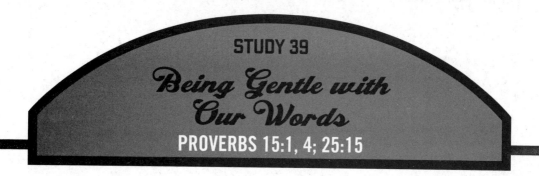

STUDY 39

Being Gentle with Our Words

PROVERBS 15:1, 4; 25:15

After twenty-five years of marriage, I am still affected (most of the time) by my husband's gentle response when I am angry. His tender words defuse a potentially explosive situation. In the proverbs we are considering in this study, we will see the power of gentle words.

WARMING UP

1. In what situations do gentle words mean the most to you?

DIGGING IN

2. Read Proverbs 15:1, 4. Verse 1 states that a gentle answer turns away wrath. When have you experienced this?

3.   When have you seen anger stirred up by harsh words?

> The Hebrew suggests [a harsh word is] one that hurts.... Gentle speech is healing, life giving; twisted speech can crush people.
>
> *The New Bible Commentary: Revised*

4.   According to verse 4, what contrasting effects can a tongue have?

5.   What do you think it means to crush someone's spirit with a perverse tongue (v. 4)?

> The nearly identical Hebrew expression in Isaiah 65:14 for a *breaking of the spirit* suggests that the effect of words on "morale" is chiefly in mind here, though it can be taken further.
>
> Derek Kidner, *Proverbs*, Tyndale Old Testament Commentaries

6. It is a sobering fact that our tongues can crush spirits. Can you think of examples when you or someone else crushed another's spirit with words? Explain.

7. How would you describe a tree of life (v. 4)? What is it like? What does it do?

The image of a tree of life is found both at the beginning of Scripture (Genesis 2:9) and at the end (Revelation 22:2). Revelation 22:2 gives a good description of the tree. The author of this proverb compares the healing of the tree to the healing of a well-spoken word.

8. When has God used your tongue for healing in another's life, or when has someone else's tongue brought you healing?

9. What steps do you need to take for your tongue to speak words of life more frequently?

10. Read Proverbs 25:15. What do patience and a gentle tongue have in common?

11. What do you think it means that a gentle tongue can break a bone?

12. How do the proverbs in this study challenge and encourage you about your words?

PRAY ABOUT IT

Confess to the Lord Jesus that sometimes you are not even aware of the effect your words have on others. Ask him to make you sensitive to how you can encourage and heal others with words and to convict you about hurtful and destructive words before you speak them.

TAKING THE NEXT STEP

Memorize and reflect daily on Proverbs 15:4. Consider how your tongue can bring healing to others. Contact at least one person every day this week to share words of encouragement and affirmation. Pray for that person that God will use your words for healing in his or her life.

I love babies. We are raising four children. Our oldest is thirteen, and the youngest is seven. We are in a new era — lots of independence and self-sufficiency. A couple of them are even taking care of other people's children. There are no more babies around. Even so, I have to admit that this is a fun period in our lives.

There are scenes, however, that still touch me deeply and cause old longings to emerge: for instance, watching a mother nurse her infant or a father teach his toddler how to play catch or kick a soccer ball. What tender pictures of love and nurture! They are precious times of security and contentment for the children and of great satisfaction for Mom and Dad. How appropriate that Paul uses the image of parenting, full of gentleness and nurture, when he describes his spiritual ministry to the Thessalonians.

WARMING UP

1. What gentle moments with your mom and dad do you remember from your childhood?

DIGGING IN

2.   Read 1 Thessalonians 2:1 – 12. What had Paul's visit to Thessalonica been like according to verses 1 – 2?

Paul's visits to Philippi and Thessalonica are described in detail in Acts 16 – 17.

3.   How would you describe Paul's motives in ministering to the Thessalonians (vv. 3 – 6)?

So many wandering religious and philosophical teachers travelled around the Roman world making what they could out of their hearers, that it was necessary for the missionaries to stress that their motives and methods were quite different from those of the less scrupulous of their rivals. The criticisms and response to them made here can be paralleled in the writings of some of the ancient philosophers who felt that they too were being unjustly accused. Basically the missionaries were charged with exploiting their followers and living at their expense.

The New Bible Commentary: Revised

4.   What usually motivates you to share the gospel and nurture other Christians?

5.   In what ways was Paul like a mother to the Thessalonians (vv. 7 – 9)?

6.   What do you think it meant that he shared not only the gospel with them but his life as well?

7.   In what ways was Paul also like a father to the Thessalonians (vv. 10 – 12)?

8.   When have other Christians treated you with motherly gentleness or fatherly care?

How did you respond to their love and concern?

9. What was the ultimate goal of Paul's ministry (v. 12)?

10. What can you do this week to encourage, comfort, or urge someone to live a life worthier of God?

How can you express gentleness in your ministry as you aim for that goal?

PRAY ABOUT IT

Thank God for specific people who have encouraged you to live a life worthy of God by gently sharing their lives and the gospel. Ask God to help you to gently share your life and the gospel with others.

TAKING THE NEXT STEP

Journal about the people in your life who have most significantly encouraged and urged you to live a life worthy of God. What characteristics and qualities did they possess? How were you specifically affected by them? How might you affect others for the kingdom by following their examples?

The Gentleness of Wisdom

JAMES 3:13–18

"Lord, please give me wisdom," I prayed as Philip and Susan ran to me in tears. Both children had their own story, and they stood before me arguing. Most of the time this type of event frustrates me as I try to get to the truth and take appropriate action. I usually walk away discouraged and defeated.

God's response to my plea came in the form of a plan of action. I calmly sent the children into a room together and told them to come out when their stories agreed. In a short time they came out, agreeing and content. All three of us experienced the gentleness of God's wisdom.

WARMING UP

1. What do you think it means to be wise?

DIGGING IN

2. Read James 3:13–18. According to verse 13, how are wisdom and understanding demonstrated?

3.   What do you think it means to live a "good life"? To be humble?

> The word James uses is *kalos*, "lovely," and what he speaks of is the loveliness of goodness, the attractiveness of the good life, its wholesomeness and helpfulness, as seen in the Lord's people: a way of life whose goodness is plain to all who see.
>
> Alec Motyer, *The Message of James*, The Bible Speaks Today

4.   How is humility an important element of being wise?

> James's own concept of humility [is] observed in three applications within his letter. Humility is, first, the teachability by which we are to accept "humbly" the word of God in 1:21. But James emphasizes there that humbly accepting God's word entails doing the word. Therefore humility is, second, a submissive readiness to do what the word says with deeds done in ... humility. Third, James shows in our current passage that in humility toward God we will become humble (and gentle) to live at peace with each other. The opposite of humility is an unwillingness to learn and a refusal to yield: the bitter envy and selfish ambition that will result in disorder.
>
> George Stulac, *James*, The IVP New Testament Commentary Series

5.   What are some characteristics of "earthly" wisdom (vv. 14 – 15)?

6.   What are the results of this kind of wisdom (v. 16)?

7.   What examples of this "earthly wisdom" and its results have you seen in our culture? In your life?

8.   How is the fruit of gentleness evident in the wisdom that comes from heaven (v. 17)?

9.   In what ways have you seen this kind of wisdom in the lives of some of the people you know?

10.   What is a "harvest of righteousness"?

Wisdom produces a good harvest. The kind of life and behavior described in this passage tends to reproduce itself. For instance, if peace permeates a local church, there will not be divisiveness.

11.   What aspects of heavenly wisdom do you most need in your life?

12.   What can you do to allow this gentle heavenly wisdom to grow more fully in you?

PRAY ABOUT IT

Praise God for heavenly wisdom—wisdom that by his power can be lived out practically in your life. Ask him to give you this wisdom. Believe that he will do it.

TAKING THE NEXT STEP

Write a letter to God. Tell him about any envy and bitterness you are harboring in your heart. Then write about any selfish ambition you are experiencing. Tell him specifically how you would like for him to replace earthly wisdom with wisdom that is from above. Describe what that would look like in your life. End the letter by thanking him for the harvest of righteousness that he is producing in you.

Gentleness and Power

2 CORINTHIANS 10:1–11

A powerful person can also be a gentle person — as Jesus himself demonstrates. But what about those who are not powerful, who are gentle in temperament as well as action? Are they disqualified from having a powerful impact on others? Must they become more macho in their ministry to be effective?

In 2 Corinthians 10 Paul is criticized by the Corinthians for being "timid," "unimpressive," and poor at public speaking. Instead of defending himself and flexing his muscles, Paul appeals to them "by the meekness and gentleness of Christ." He also shows why the world's power is powerless in spiritual warfare.

WARMING UP

1. What does the world tend to look for in a powerful person?

DIGGING IN

2. Read 2 Corinthians 10:1 – 11. How did Paul fail to measure up to the Corinthians' image of a powerful person?

Compared with the "super-apostles" (11:5) who were eloquent speakers, professionally trained in oratory, and quite impressive in person, Paul appeared to be weak, timid, and unskilled in speaking. In their eyes he was like a dog who barks at a distance but whimpers when someone comes near. What they failed to realize was that the power in Paul's ministry came from God, not Paul.

3. Why do you think he appeals to them "by the humility and gentleness of Christ" (v. 1)?

In the world of men we find nothing approaching the virtues of which Jesus spoke in the opening words of the famous Sermon on the Mount. Instead of poverty of spirit we find the rankest kind of pride; instead of meekness, arrogance; instead of hunger after righteousness we hear men saying "I am rich and increased with goods and have need of nothing"; instead of mercy we find cruelty; instead of purity of heart, corrupt imaginings; instead of peacemakers we find men quarrelsome and resentful; instead of rejoicing in mistreatment we find them fighting back with every weapon at their command.

A. W. Tozer, *The Pursuit of God*

4. What do you think Paul means when he says "we do not wage war as the world does" (v. 3)?

As [Paul's] warfare is spiritual, so the weapons with which he fights must be those bestowed by the Spirit.... The Christian will always be fighting a losing battle against temptation if he tries to fight against evil in his own strength.

R. V. G. Tasker, *The Second Epistle of Paul to the Corinthians,*
Tyndale New Testament Commentaries

5. What evidence of spiritual warfare do you see in and around you?

6. What spiritual weapons can we use to demolish the arguments and pretensions against God?

7. What does it mean to "take captive every thought to make it obedient to Christ" (v. 5)?

One of the most astonishing and undeniable arguments for the truth of the Christian religion, and for the omnipotence of God, is the fact that, when faced with the gospel, which is a scandal to the human intellect and folly to proud, unregenerate men, some of the most subtle of human intellects have been led to render submission to the Saviour. Many of the wisest have been content to become fools for Christ's sake, and not a few of the "freest" of thinkers have surrendered their "freedom" to become slaves of Him who took upon Himself the form of a servant.

Tasker, *2 Corinthians*

8. How does Paul demonstrate that gentleness is not timidity or weakness (vv. 2, 4–6, 11)?

9. How might you be inclined to defend yourself to someone who said you were "timid" and "unimpressive"?

10. Paul freely admits that his power comes not from himself but from Christ (vv. 4–5, 8). How does this give hope to those who are gentle not only in action but in temperament?

11. In review, what have you learned about the fruit of gentleness in these studies?

PRAY ABOUT IT
Ask God to make the fruit of gentleness increasingly a part of who you are in Christ.

TAKING THE NEXT STEP
In a world that sees power as external, it is difficult to live in "the humility and gentleness of Christ" (v. 1). One way to experience the power of Christ's gentleness is to "take captive every thought to make it obedient to Christ" (v. 5). Make this your goal throughout the coming week. Journal about specific thoughts you want to take captive and make obedient to Christ. How is your obedience to God affected by being aware of your thought life and turning it over to him?

Self-Control

MASTERING OUR
PASSIONS

Jack Kuhatschek

Introduction

In *The Fellowship of the Ring*, J. R. R. Tolkien describes a mysterious and magical ring with strange powers. Every person who touches the ring longs to possess it, yet finds instead that he is possessed by it.

One such person is a hobbit named Frodo. In an early scene in the book, Gandalf the wizard warns Frodo that the more the ring is used the more it enslaves the user:

> "If you had warned me," said Frodo, "or even sent me a message, I would have done away with it."
>
> "Would you?... Try!" said Gandalf. "Try now!"
>
> Frodo drew the Ring out of his pocket again and looked at it.... He had intended to fling it from him into the very hottest part of the fire. But he found now that he could not do so, not without great struggle. He weighed the Ring in his hand, hesitating, and forcing himself to remember all that Gandalf had told him; and then with an effort of will he made a movement, as if to cast it away—but he found that he had put it back in his pocket.
>
> Gandalf laughed grimly. "You see? Already you cannot easily let it go, nor will to damage it. And I could not 'make' you—except by force."[1]

Like the ring in Tolkien's story, our passions can exert a powerful influence over us. The Tempter entices us to use these good gifts in ways that God never intended. Yet the more we do so, the more they tighten their grip on us, making us slaves to their every whim.

Of course, not all of us are tempted in the same way. Some struggle with sexual passion and are lured by forbidden fruit. For others the fruit is literal—they find

---

1. J. R. R. Tolkien, *The Fellowship of the Ring* (New York: Ballantine, 1965), 93–94.

267

food of every kind irresistible and eat themselves into obesity. Others plunge themselves into debt, unable to restrain their impulse to buy anything and everything. Still others drink themselves into oblivion or take drugs to dull their awareness of a painful world. Yet in every case the warning of Scripture is clear: unless we master our passions, they will master us.

This final section of *Fruit of the Spirit* explores self-control in five crucial areas: controlling our tongue, our body, our desires, our appetites, and our finances. The last study looks at what it means to clothe ourselves with Jesus Christ.

As you look at the fruit of self-control, may God's Spirit encourage you and give you grace to master your passions.

Controlling Our Tongue

JAMES 3:1–12

Winston Churchill was known for his quick wit and sharp tongue. On one occasion, he was confronted by his archrival, Lady Astor.

"Winston," she said, "if I were your wife, I would put poison in your soup."

"Lady Astor," he replied, "if I were your husband, I would drink it!"

It's easy to laugh at such comments — especially when they aren't aimed at us. But the tongue is no laughing matter. We have all seen people utterly humiliated by a harsh word, or reduced to tears by a stinging rebuke.

In this passage James urges us to control this most uncontrollable part of our body.

WARMING UP

1.   Do you ever have difficulty controlling your tongue? Explain.

DIGGING IN

2. Read James 3:1–12. James directs his first comments at teachers and aspiring teachers (v. 1). What advice does he give them, and why?

Why do you think teachers will be judged more strictly than others?

> Because the tongue is so uncontrollable and so capable of evil, teachers bear a heavy responsibility. Their words often shape people's thinking, affect their emotions, and influence their behavior. Therefore, teachers will be judged more strictly for anything they say.

3. Why does James assume that if we can control our tongues, we must be perfect (v. 2)?

4. Do you normally think of your tongue as the most uncontrollable part of your body? Why or why not?

5.   According to James, how is the tongue like a horse's bit, a ship's rudder, and a small spark (vv. 3 – 5)?

Give examples of how your tiny tongue can direct the course of your life.

> Since *megala auchei* ("makes great boasts") is usually employed in a derogatory sense, it may be that the author uses the expression to apply the first two illustrations of the tongue's influence (vv. 3 – 4) and also to introduce the third one (vv. 5b – 6). The destructive potential of the tongue is graphically pictured by a forest fire. Thousands of acres of valuable timber may be devastated by a "small spark." In the two former illustrations, animals and ships are controlled by small objects; in this last illustration, a huge forest is destroyed by a tiny spark. The tongue likewise can either control or destroy.
>
> Donald W. Burdick, *James*, The Expositor's Bible Commentary

6.   How can the tongue's impact on people be similar to a fire (v. 6), a wild animal (vv. 7 – 8), and a deadly poison (v. 8)?

7. When have you seen a person's life hurt or even destroyed by words?

8. If "no human being can tame the tongue" (v. 8), what hope do we have of ever controlling that part of our body?

In these verses James offers very little hope of controlling our tongues. In the next paragraph, however, he does admit that we can receive a wisdom from heaven that is "pure; then peace-loving, considerate, submissive, full of mercy and good fruit, impartial and sincere" (3:17). Such qualities, which are so unnatural to the tongue, are the result of God's Spirit.

9. How does the tongue violate the laws of nature (vv. 9 – 12)?

In the natural world, a spring cannot produce both fresh water and salt, nor can a fig tree bear olives, nor a grapevine bear figs. Yet the tongue violates all laws of nature by being capable of praising God one moment and cursing others the next. James sees this as evidence of the tongue's diabolical nature.

10. How should the fact that people are made in God's likeness (v. 9) affect the way we speak to them?

11. James is very pessimistic, or perhaps realistic, about the tongue. In light of his pessimism, what advice does he give to the "wise and understanding" (see v. 13)?

Why are our deeds a better gauge of wisdom than our words?

PRAY ABOUT IT

Ask God's Spirit to put out the fire in your tongue, to tame that which is untameable, so that your speech can be appropriate for someone created in God's likeness.

TAKING THE NEXT STEP

In James 1:19 the author gives us this advice: "Take note of this: Everyone should be quick to listen, slow to speak and slow to become angry." How might this advice help you to control the impact of your tongue? What current situation are you facing in which you might put this principle into practice?

STUDY 44

Controlling Our Body

1 CORINTHIANS 6:12–20

Mae West was once told by an admirer, "Goodness, what big diamonds!"

West replied, "Goodness had nothing to do with it."

Sexual sins have always been fashionable and, for some, even a matter of pride. Yet "free sex" has never been without cost. In our day, epidemic AIDS and STDs, the horrifying abortion rate, and the agony of unwed mothers have given renewed force to the Bible's plea for sexual purity. In 1 Corinthians 6 Paul urges each of us to control our body.

WARMING UP

1.   Do you think Christians tend to be more sexually pure than non-Christians? Explain.

DIGGING IN

2. Read 1 Corinthians 6:12–20. Paul begins by countering those who say, "I have the right to do anything" (or as some translations put it, "Everything is permissible for me"). How might some Christians come to that conclusion?

> In making such claims to unrestricted freedom, some evidently used the argument that since the physical activity of eating and digesting food ... did not have any bearing on Christian morals and one's inner spiritual life, so other physical activities such as promiscuous sex did not touch either on morals or spiritual life.
>
> W. Harold Mare, *1 Corinthians*, The Expositor's Bible Commentary

3. Even if something is permissible, why might we still refrain from doing it (vv. 12–13)?

What examples can you give of permissible actions that may not be beneficial for you or might even be enslaving?

4. Some Corinthians claimed that just as the stomach was meant for food, so the body was meant for sexual immorality. According to Paul, what is wrong with their logic (vv. 13 – 14)?

5. Why should our spiritual union with Christ make sexual immorality unthinkable (vv. 15 – 17)?

Obviously, Jesus Christ is perfectly pure, holy, and sinless, and he cannot be corrupted by our sinful actions. Yet because we are members of Christ's body, whenever we sin we somehow involve the "members of Christ" in that act of sin. Paul finds that thought reprehensible, and we should too!

6. In Corinth, sexual immorality often involved temple prostitutes. What sexual temptations are we likely to encounter today?

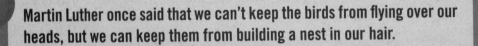

Like any large commercial city, Corinth was a center for open and unbridled immorality. The worship of Aphrodite fostered prostitution in the name of religion. At one time 1,000 sacred prostitutes served her temple. So widely known did the immorality of Corinth become that the Greek verb "to Corinthianize" came to mean "to practice sexual immorality." In a setting like this it is no wonder that the Corinthian church was plagued with numerous problems.

The NIV Study Bible

7. Paul urges us to "flee from sexual immorality" (v. 18). Why is a swift retreat usually better than a calm, rational approach to temptation?

Martin Luther once said that we can't keep the birds from flying over our heads, but we can keep them from building a nest in our hair.

8. How should the fact that our bodies are "temples of the Holy Spirit" give added force to Paul's statements (vv. 18 – 20)?

9. How would you summarize Paul's arguments for sexual purity?

10. Which of these arguments, if any, is most helpful to you? Explain.

PRAY ABOUT IT

Silently reflect on areas where you need greater sexual purity. Ask God to help you in your struggles.

TAKING THE NEXT STEP

Sometimes the best way to overcome persistent temptation is to join an accountability group. This can involve just one other person or several people. Agree to meet regularly to share your progress. Be sure to be both honest about your own struggles and supportive of others who are struggling. James urges us, "Confess your sins to each other and pray for each other so that you may be healed" (James 5:16).

STUDY 45

Controlling Our Desires

JAMES 4:1 – 10

In the book *Dr. Jekyll and Mr. Hyde*, the quiet and respectable Dr. Jekyll decides to explore the dark side of his nature. After taking a mysterious potion, he is transformed into the vile and hideous Mr. Hyde.

The author, Robert Louis Stevenson, knew that within the heart of every person lurk terrible passions and desires. Scripture tells us that "the heart is deceitful above all things and beyond cure" (Jeremiah 17:9). James confronts this dark side of our nature in chapter 4 of his letter and urges us to resist its evil influences.

WARMING UP

1.   In what situations do you tend to get angry?

DIGGING IN

2.   Read James 4:1 – 10. According to James, what causes fights and quarrels among us (vv. 1 – 2)?

3.   James speaks of desires that battle within us (vv. 1 – 2). What kinds of desires might lead people to covet and quarrel or even fight and kill?

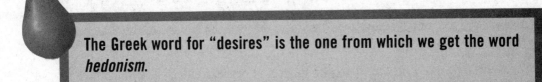

The Greek word for "desires" is the one from which we get the word *hedonism.*

4.   Why do we often fail to get what we so intensely desire (vv. 2 – 3)?

5.   Is it wrong to ask God for things that bring us pleasure? Explain.

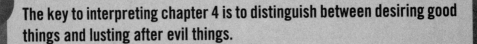

The key to interpreting chapter 4 is to distinguish between desiring good things and lusting after evil things.

6.   What does it mean to be "a friend of the world" (v. 4)?

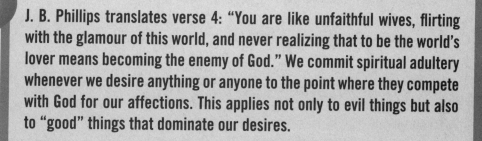

James isn't speaking of the material world that God created but rather the corrupt values that are the opposite of what God intends and the Bible teaches.

7. Why is friendship with the world a form of spiritual adultery (v. 4)?

J. B. Phillips translates verse 4: "You are like unfaithful wives, flirting with the glamour of this world, and never realizing that to be the world's lover means becoming the enemy of God." We commit spiritual adultery whenever we desire anything or anyone to the point where they compete with God for our affections. This applies not only to evil things but also to "good" things that dominate our desires.

8. Why is friendship with the world also a form of hatred and rebellion against God?

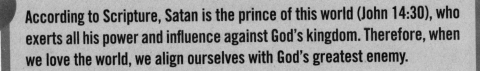

According to Scripture, Satan is the prince of this world (John 14:30), who exerts all his power and influence against God's kingdom. Therefore, when we love the world, we align ourselves with God's greatest enemy.

9. In what ways are you tempted to flirt with or even have an affair with the world?

10. What ten commandments does James give us for receiving God's grace (vv. 7 – 10)?

What is our spiritual state before and after obeying these commands?

11. What worldly desire do you struggle with most?

Why is humble submission to God the first step toward controlling that desire?

PRAY ABOUT IT

Humble yourself before the Lord. Draw near to him in prayer. Ask him for grace to purify your motives and control your desires.

TAKING THE NEXT STEP

Spend time in thought and prayer, asking the Lord to help you discern and deal with improper desires. Which desires are causing conflict with others? Which are clearly opposed to what God desires for you and others?

Controlling Our Appetites

PROVERBS 23:20–21, 29–35; 28:7

Forbidden fruit always looks sweetest — especially when you're on a diet!

You know how it goes. You're home alone, and the urge to eat seizes you. You fight it off, trying to distract yourself by reading a magazine. You "accidentally" flip to the food section, and your mouth begins to water. Feeling a twinge of guilt, you reassure yourself that pictures aren't fattening. But as you linger over each luscious page, your resistance weakens. Finally, you decide to allow yourself one chocolate-chip cookie — after all, how much damage can one cookie do? Next thing you know, the bag is empty but you are bloated!

Whether it is food, alcohol, or other drugs — controlling our appetites is never easy. Yet the book of Proverbs motivates us to master this important area of our lives.

WARMING UP

1.   What do you find hardest about dieting — or controlling any other "appetite"?

DIGGING IN

2.   Read Proverbs 23:20 – 21. What do alcoholism and gluttony have in common?

3.   It is easy to imagine how a "drunkard" could become poor (v. 21). But how could gluttony lead to poverty?

In biblical times, and in many cultures today, food was not as readily available or as inexpensive as it is in Western society. A person could, therefore, literally eat himself out of house and home. Although this is less of a threat today, gluttony still costs a considerable amount of money, which could be used for better purposes.

4.   Why do you think people who eat or drink too much rarely view themselves as gluttons or alcoholics?

5.   Read verses 29 – 35. In what ways are alcoholic beverages, such as wine, both alluring and deceptive?

6. Based on your experience or that of someone you know, how accurate is the proverb's description of what it is like to be drunk (vv. 33 – 35)?

7. What are some of the consequences of drinking too much?

   Why would alcoholism result in these consequences?

8. To what extent do the proverb's warnings against "wine" apply to other forms of addictive behavior?

9. Read Proverbs 28:7. Why do you think "a companion of gluttons" is contrasted with someone who is "discerning" and "heeds instruction"?

Gluttons are characterized by excessive, self-indulgent behavior, whereas those who keep the law are characterized by moderate, self-controlled behavior. Gluttons are not controlled by the Spirit of God but by their own appetites.

10. When it comes to our appetites, why does our behavior either show discernment or bring disgrace (v. 7)?

11. In what area would you like greater control over your appetites?

PRAY ABOUT IT

Ask God's Spirit to allow the fruit of self-control to mature in your area of weakness.

TAKING THE NEXT STEP

People who exhibit addictive behavior often have trouble admitting it. Yet being honest about our addictions — even the "small ones" — is essential to breaking free from them. If you think you might be addicted to some form of behavior, seek help from a respected friend, a support group, your pastor, or a professional counselor. Taking that step could put you on the path to greater freedom and joy.

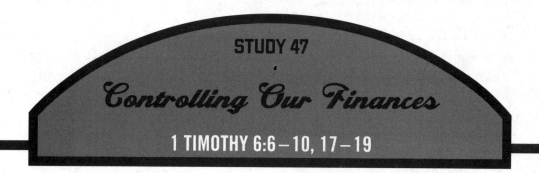

A comic strip once described how the Rockefellers made their fortune. Mrs. Rockefeller found she could save thousands of dollars each year by buying items on sale. The more items she bought on sale, the more money she saved. During the Depression, she was forced to shop seven days a week just to make ends meet!

For most of us, spending and saving don't work quite that way. We struggle to control our spending, and our savings and giving are often far less than they should be. In 1 Timothy 6 Paul helps us gain a biblical perspective on our finances.

WARMING UP

1. As people make more money, why do you think they often increase their standard of living?

DIGGING IN

2.   Read 1 Timothy 6:6 – 10. Paul tells us to be content with food and clothing (v. 8). What other material things do we often feel we need to be content?

In what ways does our culture make it difficult to be content with mere food and clothing?

3.   Paul reminds us that we brought nothing into this world, and we can take nothing out of it (v. 7). How should these facts affect our attitude toward possessions?

The words for "food" (*diatrophas*) and "clothing" (*skepasmata*) [v. 8] are both plural and are found only here in the New Testament. The ordinary word for food in the New Testament is *trophe*. But the compound occurs in the literature of that time. The term *skepasma* comes from *skepazo*, the verb meaning "to cover." So it could mean both clothing and shelter. But Josephus uses it clearly in the sense of clothing alone (*Antiquities*, xv.9.2).

Ralph Earle, *1, 2 Timothy*, The Expositor's Bible Commentary

4.   What dangers await those who want to get rich and who love money (vv. 9 – 10)?

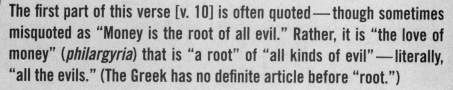

The first part of this verse [v. 10] is often quoted — though sometimes misquoted as "Money is the root of all evil." Rather, it is "the love of money" (*philargyria*) that is "a root" of "all kinds of evil" — literally, "all the evils." (The Greek has no definite article before "root.")

Earle, *1, 2 Timothy*

5.   What examples can you give of the kinds of foolish and harmful desires, evils, and griefs Paul has in mind?

6.   If the pursuit of riches is really so dangerous, why do you think so many people have made it their primary goal in life?

7.   Is your life characterized more by contentment or the love of money? Explain.

Why are these two attitudes totally incompatible?

8.   Instead of pursuing wealth, what does Paul urge Timothy and us to pursue (see v. 11)?

     Why are these qualities more valuable than riches?

9.   Read verses 17 – 19. How are those who are already rich to view themselves and their wealth (v. 17)?

10. If we put our hope in God rather than riches, does that mean we must live austere, joyless lives (v. 17)? Explain.

Although the New Testament has little good to say about money, it is wrong to conclude that God wants us to live austere, joyless lives. Paul tells us that God richly provides us with everything for our enjoyment (v. 17). Such "riches" are available to all Christians, regardless of their income.

11. How can we use our material wealth to gain true riches and treasure (vv. 18 – 19)?

12. How do your current attitudes toward money and possessions compare to the attitudes God wants you to have?

PRAY ABOUT IT

Ask God for wisdom and strength to make any changes necessary in your attitude toward money and possessions.

TAKING THE NEXT STEP

One of the best ways to break the hold that money and possessions have on us is to live generously. How might you be more generous with your money and your possessions? What step could you take this week toward becoming a more generous person?

Clothing Ourselves with Christ

ROMANS 13:11–14

King Henry II, in order to curb the growing power of the church, had a brilliant plan. He decided to nominate his good friend and chancellor, Thomas Beckett, to be archbishop of Canterbury. With Beckett as his puppet, Henry would control both church and state—or so he thought.

As the day approached for Beckett's consecration, a change came over him. When he clothed himself in the robes of the archbishop, he experienced an inner transformation. He resolved that he would not be archbishop in appearance only, but in fact—a decision that later cost him his life.

In Romans 13 Paul urges us to clothe ourselves with Christ, to resolve to be Christians not only in appearance but in the innermost parts of our being.

WARMING UP

1. How accurate is the saying "Clothes make the man"?

DIGGING IN

2.   Read Romans 13:11 – 14. What do night and day, darkness and light stand for in this passage?

3.   What words does Paul use to emphasize the nearness of Christ's return?

[This text does] not mean that the early Christians believed that Jesus would return within a few years (and thus were mistaken). Rather, they regarded the death and resurrection of Christ as the crucial events of history that began the last days. Since the next great event in God's redemptive plan is the second coming of Jesus Christ, "the night," no matter how long chronologically it may last, is "nearly over."

The NIV Study Bible, note on Romans 13:12

4.   What do the "deeds of darkness" (vv. 12 – 13) have in common?

If Paul were writing today, do you think his list of deeds in verse 13 would be the same or different? Explain.

We are to avoid ... those actions typical of the nighttime: unrestrained sexual conduct and drinking to excess (i.e., what we today call partying). Interestingly, Paul concludes his list with some unexpected items: "dissension and jealousy." He probably adds these because he is thinking ahead to the next subject he will address: the divisions in the Roman community (chapter 14).

Douglas Moo, *Romans*, The NIV Application Commentary

5.   Why do you think people are more inclined to do such deeds in the darkness rather than in the light?

6.   What does it mean to "clothe yourselves with the Lord Jesus Christ" (v. 14)?

This amounts to appropriation—the deliberate, conscious acceptance of the lordship of the Master—so that all is under his control—motives, desires, and deeds. A slight difficulty meets us at this point, since believers have already put on Christ, according to Galatians 3:27, at conversion and baptism. But there is always room for decisive renewal, for fresh advance.

Everett F. Harrison, *Romans*, The Expositor's Bible Commentary

Paul also speaks of our putting on "the armor of light" (v. 12). What does that idea add to the image of clothing?

> By using the imagery of armor (see also Ephesians 6:10–18; 1 Thessalonians 5:1–11), Paul alerts us to the fact that as we walk through the world we must be prepared for combat with the powers of darkness, who have already been defeated by Christ but who are unwilling to concede his victory.

7. If Paul had made a list of Christlike clothes to put on, what might that list have included (see, for example, vv. 8–10)?

8. Which items in that list are most absent from your wardrobe?

9. What is one practical way you might clothe yourself with those qualities?

10. If we clothe ourselves with Jesus Christ, why is it wrong even to think about gratifying our sinful desires (v. 14)?

We cannot follow both the Spirit and the sinful nature at the same time, because they lead in opposite directions!

11. How does the dawning of Christ's return motivate you to "dress" differently than you might otherwise?

PRAY ABOUT IT

Thank God for the passing of night and the nearness of day. Ask him to help you dress in clothes fit for the occasion.

TAKING THE NEXT STEP

You may love to shop for clothes — or you may hate to. Yet clearly the Lord wants you to invest in a new moral wardrobe. Spend time in prayer, Bible study, and reflection, asking him to show you what new clothes you should acquire and put on.

Faith Lessons Series

Walking with God in the Desert Discovery Guide with DVD

Ray Vander Laan with Stephen and Amanda Sorenson

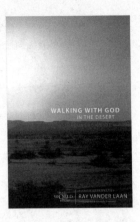

Filmed on location in the Middle East, Faith Lessons is a unique video series that brings God's Word to life with astounding relevance. By weaving together the Bible's fascinating historical, cultural, religious, and geographical contexts, teacher and historian Ray Vander Laan reveals keen insights into the Scriptures' significance for modern believers. These illuminating "faith lessons" afford a new understanding of the Bible that will ground your convictions and transform your life. The Faith Lessons video series (each available with a discovery guide that includes discussion questions, maps, photos, and in-depth personal studies) is ideal for use at home, especially in personal and family Bible studies. Individual believers and families will gain vital insights from long-ago times and cultures through this innovative approach to Bible study.

The seven sessions of *Walking with God in the Desert* include:

1. Join the Journey
2. It's Hot in Here and There's No Way Out
3. Help Is Here
4. When Your Heart Cries Out
5. They Were Not Wandering
6. Ears to Hear
7. There's Hope in the Desert

Available in stores and online!

Share Your Thoughts

With the Author: Your comments will be forwarded to the author when you send them to *zauthor@zondervan.com*.

With Zondervan: Submit your review of this book by writing to *zreview@zondervan.com*.

Free Online Resources at

www.zondervan.com

Zondervan AuthorTracker: Be notified whenever your favorite authors publish new books, go on tour, or post an update about what's happening in their lives at www.zondervan.com/authortracker.

Daily Bible Verses and Devotions: Enrich your life with daily Bible verses or devotions that help you start every morning focused on God. Visit www.zondervan.com/newsletters.

Free Email Publications: Sign up for newsletters on Christian living, academic resources, church ministry, fiction, children's resources, and more. Visit www.zondervan.com/newsletters.

Zondervan Bible Search: Find and compare Bible passages in a variety of translations at www.zondervanbiblesearch.com.

Other Benefits: Register yourself to receive online benefits like coupons and special offers, or to participate in research.

ZONDERVAN®

ZONDERVAN.com/
AUTHORTRACKER
follow your favorite authors